W9-ABY-942

Sociology of
American Indians

BIBLIOGRAPHICAL SERIES
*The Newberry Library Center
for the History of the American Indian*

General Editor
Francis Jennings

Assistant Editor
William R. Swagerty

The Center Is Supported by Grants from

The National Endowment for the Humanities
The Ford Foundation
The W. Clement and Jessie V. Stone Foundation
The Woods Charitable Fund, Inc.
Mr. Gaylord Donnelley
The Andrew W. Mellon Foundation
The Robert R. McCormick Charitable Trust
The John D. and Catherine T. McArthur Foundation

Sociology of American Indians

A Critical Bibliography

RUSSELL THORNTON

AND

MARY K. GRASMICK

Published for the Newberry Library

Indiana University Press

BLOOMINGTON

Manufactured in the United States of America

Library of Congress Cataloging in Publication Data

Thornton, Russell, 1942–
  Sociology of American Indians.

  (Bibliographical series)
  Includes index.
  1.Indians of North America—Social conditions—Bibliography. 2.Indians of North America—Bibliography.
I.Grasmick, Mary K., 1953– joint author. II.Title. III.Series.
Z1209.T46 [E98.S67] 016.3058'97073 80–8035
ISBN 0–253–35294–0 (pkb.) 1 2 3 4 5 84 83 82 81 80

CONTENTS

ACKNOWLEDGMENTS

Early work in the preparation of this bibliography was supported by funds from the Center for Urban and Regional Affairs at the University of Minnesota. Special appreciation for this support is extended to the Center's director, Tom Scott, and associate director, Tom Anding. Research assistance was provided initially by Lois Marsh Shamat and later by Melissa Meyer. Tim Dunnigan provided valuable editorial suggestions. The final draft of the bibliography was completed during the senior author's tenure under a Research Scientist Career Development Award from the National Institute of Mental Health.

RECOMMENDED WORKS

For the Beginner

[16]   Howard M. Bahr, Bruce A. Chadwick, and
        Robert C. Day, eds., *Native Americans Today:
        Sociological Perspectives.*

[106]   Jeanne Guillemin, *Urban Renegades: The Cul-
        tural Strategy of American Indians.*

[282]   Russell Thornton and Mary K. Grasmick,
        "Sociological Study of American Indians: A
        Research Note on Journal Literature."

[299]   Albert L. Wahrhaftig and Robert K. Thomas,
        "Renaissance and Repression: The Oklahoma
        Cherokee."

[309]   Murray L. Wax, *Indian Americans: Unity and Di-
        versity.*

For a Basic Library Collection

[28]   Ann H. Beuf, *Red Children in White America.*

[42]   Niels Winther Braroe, *Indian and White: Self-
        Image and Interaction in a Canadian Plains Com-
        munity.*

[94]   Estelle Fuchs and Robert J. Havighurst, *To Live
        on This Earth: American Indian Education.*

[121]   Robert J. Havighurst and Bernice L. Neugarten, *American Indian and White Children: A Sociopsychological Investigation.*

[162]   Forrest E. LaViolette, *The Struggle for Survival: Indian Cultures and the Protestant Ethic in British Columbia.*

[216]   Jeffrey Passel, "Provisional Evaluation of the 1970 Census Count of American Indians."

[250]   George E. Simpson and J. Milton Yinger, eds., "American Indians and American Life."

[258]   Alan L. Sorkin, *The Urban American Indian.*

[285]   Ronald L. Trosper, "Native American Boundary Maintenance: The Flathead Indian Reservation, Montana, 1860–1970."

[297]   Jack O. Waddell and O. Michael Watson, eds., *The American Indian in Urban Society.*

[298]   Albert L. Wahrhaftig, "The Tribal Cherokee Population of Eastern Oklahoma."

[310]   Murray L. Wax and Robert W. Buchanan, eds., *Solving "The Indian Problem": The White Man's Burdensome Business.*

[312]   Murray L. Wax, Rosalie H. Wax, and Robert V. Dumont, Jr., "Formal Education in an American Indian Community."

BIBLIOGRAPHICAL ESSAY

Why Sociology of American Indians?

This bibliography departs in an important way from others published in the Newberry Library Center for the History of the American Indian Bibliographical Series. Previous bibliographies have been on specific topics such as historical demography, Indian missions, and United States Indian policy, or on tribes of various regions such as the Plains, the Northeast, and California, or on individual tribes such as the Apaches, the Cherokees, and the Ojibwas. The present bibliography is not restricted to any particular topic or region or tribe. It is, however, restricted to the sociological literature. Thus a consideration of the importance of this discipline to a knowledge of American Indians seems appropriate at the onset.

Imbalance in the Study of American Indians

We recently surveyed the literature of the social science disciplines for articles pertaining to American Indians. The largest number of articles—several thousand—are published in anthropological journals, and another fifteen hundred appear in history journals. The journals in economics and political science contain only a few dozen articles each. American studies, ethnic studies, and geography each have approximately a hundred articles on American Indians. The sociological literature contains about three hundred relevant articles produced in the almost one-hundred-year history of sociology in the United States and Canada. (See our *Bibliography of Social Science Research and Writings on American Indians* [281] and "Sociological Study of American Indians: A Research Note on Journal Literature" [282] for more complete and detailed information.)

Implications of Imbalance for Society and for American Indians

This disciplinary imbalance carries important implications, strongly suggesting the need for more study of American Indians by disciplines other than anthropology or history. The strong emphasis on traditional cultures in the scholarly publications of both anthropology and history has been very influential in shaping public knowledge. Other social science disciplines are concerned primarily with contemporary peoples, but they have not studied American Indians to any extent. Consequently, the knowledge of the social sciences and, by implication, of American society is biased toward American Indians as members of traditional and historical cultures rather than as modern, contemporary peoples.

Any social science discipline may be viewed as a set of topics or issues of (generally) long-standing concern that are more or less particular to it and distinguish it from other disciplines. Examples are the study of kinship systems in anthropology, social class in sociology, and voting behavior in political science. The far greater study of American Indians in anthropology and history than in other social sciences has led to emphasis on issues of interest to these disciplines and neglect of those of interest to geographers, economists, political scientists, and sociologists. For instance, we know a fair amount about the structure of kinship relations among different tribes because of the long-standing interest of anthropologists in the topic, but we know very little about family structure or the dynamics of family life among different tribes because sociologists of the family have lacked interest in American Indians.

Implications of Imbalance for Sociology

This imbalance also has implications for sociology as a discipline. Even in the publications of sociology, treatments of American Indians tend to be distinctly anthropological or historical in nature and authorship. This was particularly true in the last decade of the nineteenth century and the first few decades of the twentieth. William I. Thomas's two publications of the late 1890s, "The Relation of Sex to Primitive Social Control" [273] and "Sex in Primitive Industry" [274], both contain examples from American Indian groups and were published in the *American Journal of Sociology*. But both are more anthropological than sociological. Two other early publications on American Indians in the *American Journal of Sociology*, written by Robert H. Lowie, must also be considered not sociological but anthropological. "Cultural Anthropology: A Science" [168] is in no way concerned with sociology, and "Psychology and Sociology" [167], which is presented as a discussion of the possible contributions of psychology to sociology in studying American Indians, refers more to anthropology than to sociology. Similarly, neither Bernhard J. Stern's paper in *Social Forces* discussing "Lewis Henry Morgan: American Ethnologist" [264], nor Henry S. Spalding's "The Ethnologic Value of the Jesuit Relations" [259] refers to what may be considered sociology per se.

Sociology grew in part from anthropology, and a strong anthropological orientation was to be expected in its early literature. But this continues to be the case when the subject matter concerns American Indians. Walter Goldschmidt's "Values and the Field of Comparative Sociology" [100] is an attempt to illustrate the usefulness of anthropology to the development of sociological theory, using American Indian cultures as examples. June Helm's "The Ecological Approach in Anthropology" [126] also considers American Indians and anthropology. Both of these are contemporary publications, the former published in the *American Sociological Review* in 1953 and the latter in the *American Journal of Sociology* in 1962.

The extent of contemporary sociology's reliance on history and anthropology may be seen in two relatively recent review essays of books on American Indians. Of the six books reviewed by Murray L. Wax in his *Social Problems* paper "The White Man's Burdensome 'Business': A Review Essay on the Change and Constancy of Literature on the American Indians" [308], not one was written by a sociologist as far as we could tell. Primarily, the authors were anthropologists and historians. Similarly, historians and anthropologists wrote most of the five books reviewed by the sociologists Howard M. Bahr and Bruce A. Chadwick in "Contemporary Perspectives on American Indians: A Review Essay" [14], published in *Social Science Quarterly*.

We are not advocating the isolation of disciplines, since there are many benefits to their interpenetration.

The point is that the bias toward anthropology and history finds its way into the literature of sociology, so that discussions of American Indians within sociology often seem to go hand in hand with anthropology or history.

The Importance of Sociology in the Study of American Indians

Anthropology and history are certainly excellent disciplines within which to study American Indians, and much knowledge about the subject has come out of them. Other social science disciplines—economics, geography, political science, and psychology—are also appropriate, as is sociology. (For a discussion of some issues involved in this study, see Russell Thornton's "American Indian Studies as an Academic Discipline" [278].) Sociology has a somewhat broader mandate than other social science disciplines, however, and consequently could perhaps contribute more toward balancing the study of American Indians.

Sociology's focus on human societies, their subsystems, and their patterns of interaction differs significantly from the more cultural concerns of anthropology. The preference in sociology for contemporary, urban societies is needed to complement both the chronological concerns of history and anthropology's emphasis on traditional and rural cultures. For example, sociology's interest in the family unit is just as important as anthropology's interest in the kinship systems of American Indians, and sociology's concern with social stratification would provide new perspectives on past events in the history of American Indian–White relations.

Sociology thus has great potential for providing knowledge of modern American Indians to complement knowledge of traditional, historical Indian peoples. This balance would also enhance American Indians' understanding of themselves in contemporary American society, for they also often depend upon general societal knowledge for information about themselves.

These same "needs" were discussed in the early part of this century when sociology was just starting to develop. In "The Assimilation of the American Indian" [175, p. 771], Fayette Avery McKenzie called on sociology to give increased attention to problems and concerns of contemporary American Indians:

> We have eminent professors who as anthropologists, ethnologists, and historians study the Indian of the past. Should we not have men who can devote themselves to the problem of the Indian as he now is, and to the problems of the means by which he may realize his highest possibilities as a citizen and fellow worker? Such studies should mean vast things, not only for the United States, but for the uncounted millions of native Americans in the countries to the south of us. The nation and the continent call for this great new chair in sociology. Do we not owe this to people we have so largely dispossessed?

Sixty-five years later, it is obvious that McKenzie's plea has had little influence on sociology.

Aside from benefits to society at large and to American Indian peoples, sociology itself would benefit if it were to intensify its study of American Indians. Though sociology has a tradition of studying minority groups within American society, its knowledge of these groups is dominated by a concentration on Black Americans to the virtual exclusion of other groups. In

"The Sociological Study of Minority Groups as Reflected by Leáding Sociology Journals: Who Gets Studied and Who Gets Neglected?" [161], Abraham D. Lavender and John M. Forsyth find that more than 70 percent of the articles on intergroup relations in the history of the three leading sociology journals (*American Journal of Sociology, American Sociological Review,* and *Social Forces*) dealt with Blacks. No more than 6 percent considered any one other group, and fewer than 5 percent considered American Indians.

The extent to which knowledge of Black Americans may be generalized to any other group is, of course, problematic. It would be extremely difficult to generalize it (or knowledge of any other minority group) to American Indians because Indians are unique in their relationship to American society, with a separate legal status. Some American Indian peoples also have cultures still partially "freestanding"; that is, cultures separated from larger American culture, able in many respects to exist without it.

Since American Indians are unique, they present new conceptual and theoretical challenges that would stimulate growth within the discipline and extend its methodological base. There are few if any topics of interest to sociologists that could not be examined using as subjects American Indians or American Indian groups. This is as true for the study of the sociological concepts as "role," "status equilibrium," and "social networks" as it is for more concrete sociological interests such as educational attainment, marriage patterns, and migration. Using American Indians to study social phenomena on various levels of abstraction would be not only appropriate but heuristic.

Inclusions and Omissions

Selecting publications for inclusion in this bibliography required prior definition of both "sociological literature" and "on American Indians." We defined "sociological literature" as books and journal articles on sociological concerns or with a sociological focus. This definition includes many materials written by scholars trained in areas other than sociology. We consider relevant all books and journals published in the United States and Canada irrespective of publication date. "On American Indians" means any type of discussion of American Indians, American Indian tribes, or explicit American Indian concerns, or the inclusion of American Indians or American Indian tribes as a distinct comparative facet of a sample. Works covering Eskimos and Aleuts are included, as are works on other native peoples of Canada.

Given our definitions, there are more than three hundred sociological journal articles on American Indians but only a few books, some of which are merely collections of previously published articles. Most of these have been written by sociologists, but a significant number of the authors are anthropologists. We have included virtually all the articles and books we located.

Occasionally it was difficult to decide whether a particular work fit our criteria. We have rejected as few works as possible, but we have, however, purposely excluded all theses and other unpublished materials. We hope the bibliography may be considered an enumeration and discussion of the virtual totality of the history of American sociological study of American Indians as here defined.

There is a small body of partially relevant work that utilizes American Indians as part of a broader cross-cultural sample or data set but is not concerned with them per se and does not include them as an explicit comparative facet of the sample. In ten instances, however, American Indians are specified as included, usually constituting from one-fifth to one-fourth of the sample or data set. These ten works—two books and eight articles—may be of interest to the reader and are enumerated here. The books are Stanley H. Udy, Jr.'s *Organization of Work* [288] and Alvin W. Gouldner and Richard A. Peterson's *Notes on Technology and the Moral Order* [101]. The articles are Walter T. Watson's "A New Census and an Old Theory: Division of Labor in the Preliterate World" [306]; Julia S. Brown's "A Comparative Study of Deviations from Sexual Mores" [45]; James G. March's "Group Autonomy and Intergroup Control" [187]; Karen E. Paige and Jeffrey M. Paige's "The Politics of Birth Practices: A Strategic Analysis" [209]; Stanley H. Udy, Jr.'s, "'Bureaucratic' Elements in Organizations: Some Research Findings" [287]; Mark Abrahamson's "Correlates of Political Complexity" [4]; Paul C. Rosenblatt's "Communication in the Practice of Love Magic" [235]; and Hornell Hart and Donald L. Taylor's "Was There a Prehistoric Trend from Smaller to Larger Political Units?" [116].

Demography of American Indians

We have divided sociological studies of American Indian populations into two classes on the basis of a historical or contemporary time reference. Studies of historical populations encompass the pre-Columbian state, the effects of initial European contact, and the long-term changes since the first European contact. Studies of contemporary populations include considerations of health statistics, fertility behavior, intermarriage, and problems of definition and enumeration.

Historical Indian Populations

Sociological work in American Indian historical demography dates back several decades. The two earliest articles in the sociological literature were published in 1934, and both focused on the effect of European contact on American Indian populations. In "The Aborigines of Southern California" [130], Edgar L. Hewett compares the relatively strong survival of the Indian populations in the Southwest with the virtual destruction of Indian populations in southern California. According to Hewett, these differences may be explained in terms of the greater strength of the cultural heritage of the tribes of the Southwest. The article is, however, only a discussion of these differences, with no real documentation. A not particularly useful essay is Glen E. Carlson's "The American Indian—Past and Present" [50], a loose discussion of pre-Columbian population estimates and of the effects of European and American policies on the number and distribution of American Indians. Carlson also gives his own estimates of twentieth-century population sizes. Considerably more substantial is Burt W. Aginsky's "Population Control in the Shanel (Pomo) Tribe" [6]. This is an informative discussion of various traditional means of birth control practiced by this segment of the Pomo in northern California, and of their influence on current contraceptive behavior.

General overviews of changes in American Indian populations since European contact are provided by Edward Nelson Palmer, J. Nixon Hadley, and Brewton Berry. "Culture Contacts and Population Growth" [210], by Palmer, contains a very general discussion of effects and changes resulting from European contact with native populations throughout the world. Hadley's "Demography of American Indians" [111] is an informative and concise overview of the history of the American Indian population. It describes changes in population size and discusses various reasons for the decimation of American Indians between initial European contact and the end of the nineteenth century. Hadley also covers current characteristics of the Indian population, possible future trends, and the problems of obtaining an accurate enumeration. The paper would be extremely useful for someone seeking a general overview of the American Indian population, though its description of the current population is now dated. (An update of this paper, taking particular note of information from the 1970 census, is Sam Stanley and Robert K. Thomas, "Current Social and Demographic Trends among North American Indians" [262].) Berry's "The Myth of the Vanishing Indian" [27] provides an overview of population changes as well as a discussion of the difficulties of enumeration that have been a problem for demographers studying American Indian populations. Berry refers to what he calls the "myth" of American Indian population destruction, stressing twentiety-century population gains rather than the preceding tremendous population decline.

A variety of papers on the history of American Indian populations were published during the 1970s. In G. Edward Stephan and Stephen M. Wright's "Indian Tribal Territories in the Pacific Northwest: A Cross-Cultural Test of the Size-Density Hypothesis" [263], estimates of aboriginal populations and territories are used as a cross-cultural sample to support the hypothesis that spatial size varies inversely with population density. Jane Riblett Wilkie's "The United States Population by Race and Urban-Rural Residence 1790–1860: Reference Tables" [318] provides 1860 figures for American Indians as well as a valuable summary of data for other populations in the United States.

William Peterson provides a critical discussion of demographic research on prehistoric populations, including those of American Indians, in "A Demographer's View of Prehistoric Demography" [218]. It is a strong and somewhat controversial criticism of much of this work and calls for the improvement of techniques for the analysis of sparse data. It and the accompanying comments by other demographers, especially those by Henry F. Dobyns, are useful to students of prehistoric and historic Indian populations.

Russell Thornton has recently published two papers in American Indian historical demography. "Implications of Catlin's American Indian Population Estimates for Revision of Mooney's Estimate" [279] reports the previously ignored population estimates George Catlin made for forty-one tribes in the 1830s and compares them with estimates provided in Mooney's classic study [197]. Thornton supports the current upward revisions of Mooney's figures. Demographic methods and objectives are discussed by Thornton in "American Indian Historical Demography: A Review Essay with Suggestions for Future Research" [280]. For more references in this field, see *Native American Historical Demography: A Critical Bibliography* [78] by Henry F. Dobyns in this series.

Contemporary Indian Populations

Sociological interest in the contemporary demography of American Indians dates to the early part of this century. The need for reliable health and vital statistics was stressed by Joseph A. Murphy in his 1911 article "Health Problems of the Indians" [200]. John Adair, Kurt Deuschle, and Walsh McDermott provide an informative overview of the health situation of the Navajos in the 1950s in "Patterns of Health and Disease among the Navahos" [5]. Their attempt to describe health facilities and problems within the context of Navajo culture, life-style, and religious beliefs regarding health is commendable. Patricia D. Mail, in "Hippocrates Was a Medicine Man: The Health Care of Native Americans in the Twentieth Century" [185], gives particular attention to the Indian Health Service and its effect on the health of American Indians during the past twenty-five years. Focusing on the Navajos as well as the Hopis, Stephen J. Kunitz accounts for population differences between the two tribes on the basis of federal policies and, to a lesser degree, living arrangements in his "Factors Influencing Recent Navajo and Hopi Population Change" [154].

The Papagos have been the subjects of several demographic studies. Robert A. Hackenberg's "An Anthropological Study of the Demographic Transition: The Papago Information System" [110] details problems in gathering contemporary longitudinal data on

Indian populations. It contains a description of planned development of a demographic information system as a means of studying the demographic transition hypothesis. C. Roderick Wilson also focuses on the Papagos in "Papago Indian Population Movement: An Index of Culture Change" [320]. Herman A. Tyroler and Ralph Patrick, in "Epidemiologic Studies of Papago Indian Mortality" [286], use data from the Arizona State Department of Health to examine vital rates and causes of death for the Papagos from 1950 to 1959. Surprisingly, they find both birth rates and death rates higher in modern than in traditional villages. Inadequacies in reporting systems are also discussed. Finally, Julie M. Uhlmann discusses "The Impact of Modernization upon Papago Indian Fertility" [289].

"The Tribal Cherokee Population of Eastern Oklahoma" [298], by Albert L. Wahrhaftig, is a good account of one of the larger, and in many ways more traditional, American Indian peoples of today. The data, collected in 1963, provide a great deal of information about the tribal Cherokees in Adair, Cherokee, Delaware, Sequoyah, and Mayes counties, Oklahoma. Issues of enumeration and identification in Mexico are discussed by Bernice A. Kaplan in "Ethnic Identification in an Indian Mestizo Community" [148].

Two early studies in this decade focus on problems of obtaining demographic data on native populations in Canada, where there seems to be more interest in such issues than in the United States. A. Romaniuk and Victor Piche's "Natality Estimates for the Canadian Indians by Stable Population Models, 1900–1969" [234] is a solid effort at calculating trustworthy estimates for Indian birthrates using two indirect methods, one based on age distribution data, the other on children ever born to women, by age. Fertility patterns during this period are tabulated and discussed. "Estimates of Vital Rates for the Canadian Indians, 1960–1970" [221], by Victor Piche and M. V. George, evaluates a set of registered data on Canadian Indians, offering vital rates for the decade using data corrected for inconsistencies in birth reporting.

Two other articles also consider fertility. "Modernization and Fertility: The Case of the James Bay Indians" [233], by A. Romaniuk, reports a demographic survey of Cree Indians as a test of the theory that early stages of modernization often produce increased fertility through easing restrictions on procreative behavior. The findings are that in fact fertility did increase, and Romaniuk claims support for the theory. The study "Value of Children and Fertility Behavior in a Tri-Racial, Rural County" [284], by Patricia L. Tobin, William B. Clifford, R. David Mustian, and A. Clarke Davis, examines the fertility behavior of American Indians as well as that of Whites and Blacks in a rural county in North Carolina. Both desired and actual fertility are measured against people's idea of the value of children. American Indians showed the greatest consistency between value of children and fertility, both desired and actual.

Two articles from the Population Research Laboratory of the University of Alberta report differentials in age at first marriage for Canadian ethnic groups, including Indians and Eskimos. These are "Ethnic Differentials in Age at First Marriage, Canada 1961" [224], by Indira I. Reddy and P. Krishnan, and "Ethnic Differentials in Age at First Marriage, Canada 1971" [76], by Barbara DeRuyter.

Intermarriage in a United States urban population

is the focus of Constantine Panunzio's "Intermarriage in Los Angeles, 1924–33" [212] and John H. Burma's "Interethnic Marriage in Los Angeles, 1948–1959" [48]. Both studies contain data on American Indian–other marriages, though the main focus is on non-Indian groups.

Jeffrey S. Passel's "Provisional Evaluation of the 1970 Census Count of American Indians" [216] presents a convincing explanation for the large increase in the American Indian population between 1960 and 1970 as measured by the 1960 and 1970 censuses. The difference between the census total and the lower figure one would expect from natural increase is 67,000. Passel argues that many individuals counted as White in the 1960 census shifted their self-identification to American Indian before the 1970 census.

Sociocultural Change

The publications on sociocultural change are divided into three categories: broad overviews of American Indian societies and cultures and their histories; studies of sociocultural changes resulting from European contacts; and works that analyze Indian responses to change.

Overviews

These overviews of Indian societies and cultures and their histories are either descriptive or theoretical accounts of precontact American Indian peoples. Two articles published in the late 1920s discuss distinguishing features of American Indian cultures. The first is

E. B. Renaud's "Evolution of Population and Dwelling in the Indian Southwest" [225], which uses mostly archaeological evidence to describe "cultural periods" in the Southwest before Spanish contact. The second is Russell Gordon Smith's "The Concept of the Cultural Area" [253], a discussion using examples from North America.

Three more contemporary publications also contain discussions of American Indian cultures. In "Themes as Dynamic Forces in Culture" [207], Morris Edward Opler discusses the "themes" serving to control behavior and stimulate activity among the Chiricahua Apaches. In "Symbolism in Totem Poles" [38], Emory S. Bogardus describes and interprets six types of totem poles as facets of Indian culture, and in "Social Life of the Cliff Dwellers" [39] he describes aspects of Hopi traditional life.

Karl F. Schuessler and Harold Driver's "A Factor Analysis of Sixteen Primitive Societies" [242] is a methodologically oriented report of an analysis of selected traits—for example, housing, crime, marriage, and ceremonies—of California Indian peoples. Schuessler and Driver emphasize the utility of this type of analysis for anthropological research.

Changes

Jennings J. Rhyne describes change in an Oklahoma Indian community in "Community Organization in an Indian Settlement" [227]. The relative lack of community participation among the Big Jim Band of Absentee Shawnee, according to Rhyne, reflects the disorganized state of their social relations.

In "Personal Conflicts and Cultural Change" [20], H. G. Barnett depicts the history of intercultural contact of the Yuroks, Hupas, and Karoks of northwestern California. His principal thesis is that the tribal members who were the primary adopters of White culture were also tribal misfits who were repudiated rather than followed.

The nature of intergenerational breakdown during social change is the topic of two papers: Norman S. Hayner and Una Hayner's report on tribes in the Pacific Northwest, "Three Generations of Pacific Northwest Indians" [124], and Bernard J. Siegel's report of research among the Picuris Pueblo, "Social Disorganization in Picuris Pueblo" [247].

Along this same line are two other papers, one on the Hopis and one on the Eastern Cherokees. "White Pressures on Indian Personality and Culture" [277], by Laura Thompson and Alice Joseph, contains a comparison of the patterns of change in two Hopi communities that illustrates the disruptive effects of Catholic missions on the ceremonial cycle and consequently on the entire community. "The Acculturation of Eastern Cherokee Community Organization" [107], by John Gulick, is a summary of the historical processes leading to a loss of *Gemeinschaft,* or community feeling, in an Eastern Cherokee community in North Carolina.

The next four articles on sociocultural change were published in the 1960s. John D. Photiadis analyzes the effect of federal agencies on Dakota society in his "Critical Examination of Change Programs in the Light of a System in Equilibrium" [220]. Political conflicts and their historical antecedents within a changing community are the focus of James A. Clifton's "Cultural

Change, Structural Stability, and Factionalism in the Prairie Potawatomi Reservation Community" [58]. The other two articles focus on the process of modernization in Canadian Indian communities. In "Modernism and the Hinterland: The Canadian Example" [65], Ronald Cohen discusses the relative impact of modernization on three northern Canadian communities. In "Modernization among Town and Bush Cree in Quebec" [134], David E. W. Holden considers social-psychological accompaniments to modernization when comparing the relationship of change in role structure and attitude among different groups of Crees.

Differing somewhat from other literature reviewed in this section are three comparative papers. In "Civilization and Its Effect on Indian Character" [199], E. E. Muntz discusses the diverse nature of tribal mores and questions the common belief that European contact had a "contaminating" influence on what may be called "Indian character." Robert H. Lowie draws from American Indian history in a discussion of the nature of societal dynamics that emphasizes that indigenous change as well as change from cultural contact is characteristic of native societies. The title of his paper is "The Transition of Civilizations in Primitive Societies" [169]. Examples from Chinese and American Indian societies are used in Morton H. Fried's "Land Tenure, Geography, and Ecology in the Contact of Cultures" [93], which examines the importance of a society's environmental relationships to its stability when in contact with other, expanding societies.

Responses

American Indian peoples have exhibited various responses to the deterioration of their cultures and societies since contact with Europeans. Our discussion of the sociological literature on such responses is organized around the topics of *cultural renascence* — that is, cultural revival; *cultural retention* — the retaining of cultural traits and patterns in the face of change; and *cultural adaptation* — the accommodation or modification of cultural characteristics to prevent their complete loss.

The concept of cultural renascence has been used by two authors of sociological papers on American Indians. Harriet J. Kupferer uses it in her study "The Isolated Eastern Cherokee" [157]. She concludes that the Eastern Cherokees of the early 1960s were not undergoing the renascence characteristic of many other tribes. She offers three reasons: the isolation of the Eastern Cherokees from other Indians; the absence of threats to the continuation of their reservation; and a relatively prosperous and secure economy. In a somewhat similar case, Deward Walker concludes the Nez Perces were not undergoing a cultural renascence at the time of his study in the early 1960s, with the possible exception of a limited renascence in the political area. His paper is entitled "Some Limitations of the Renascence Concept in Acculturation: The Nez Perce Case" [300].

Three papers discuss native art forms as mechanisms for cultural retention. An early article by Odd S. Halseth, "The Revival of Pueblo Pottery Making" [114], describes the cultural and economic benefits that have accrued to the Pueblo Indians from their revival of pottery craftsmanship. In "Alaskan Native Social Adjustment and the Role of Eskimo and Indian Music" [143], Thomas F. Johnston discusses Alaskan Eskimo and Tlingit traditional music as a mechanism for maintaining cultural identities in a context of rapid social change resulting from White contact. "The Eskimo and 'Airport Art'" [102], by Nelson Graburn, points out that Eskimo soapstone carving is an economic rather than a cultural enterprise, inasmuch as it is only a few decades old.

One form of response to cultural deterioration is the attempt to adapt or defend cultural elements so they are not lost completely. Bernard J. Siegel has written two articles on such adaptations. "High Anxiety Levels and Cultural Integration: Notes on a Psychocultural Hypothesis" [246] describes the Hopis as an example of a culture that has created internalized controls and ceremonial heads to regulate behavior to assure group survival. "Defensive Structuring and Environmental Stress" [248] is an analysis of the Taos and Picuris pueblos as examples of cultures that have adopted "defensive structuring"—authoritarian control, high rate of endogamy, cultivation of identity symbols, and early learning of impulse control—as a means of coping with environmental stress. Robert J. Dryfoos, Jr., in "Two Tactics for Ethnic Survival: Eskimo and Indian" [80], examines why Eskimos have adapted more readily to Euro-Canadian culture than have the Indians. He explains this difference in terms of the Eskimos being less interested in their past.

The general issue of survival through adaptation is the topic of Forrest E. LaViolette's interesting work *The*

Struggle for Survival: Indian Cultures and the Protestant Ethic in British Columbia [162]. Special emphasis is placed on the institution of potlatching and on attempts to eliminate it legally. There is also considerable discussion of the "land title question." This book is a good study of some of the threats that have been faced by all Indian peoples and of their responses to them. In "Identity, Militancy, and Cultural Congruence: The Menominee and Kainai" [261], George D. Spindler and Louise Spindler illustrate how two Indian peoples differ in their adaptive responses to confrontation with Western culture.

Religion and Religious Movements

There is a small group of publications pertaining to religion within the sociological literature on American Indians, and a large number of works may be classified under the more general rubric of "religious movements." We discuss both groups here.

Religion

Ruth Underhill's "Religion among American Indians" [292] considers American Indian religion both before and since contact with Europeans. It is a concise, informative overview of traditional elements of Indian religions and of the carryover of these elements into post-European Indian religions such as the Peyote Cult and the Native American Church. Murray L. Wax and Rosalie Wax provide a similar view in their recent "Religion among American Indians" [311]. Mary Watters, in "The Penitentes: A Folk-Observance" [307], touches on some traditional elements of Indian religion in her description of a religious observance in the Southwest that reflects a mixture of Indian traditions and Spanish Catholicism. More concerned with contemporary religion are Florence Hawley's description of an Indian family's conversion to a Black Pentecostal church in "The Keresan Holy Rollers: An Adaption to American Individualism" [122] and Robert K. Thomas's "The Role of the Church in Indian Adjustment" [272].

Religious Movements

Publications on what we call religious movements cover a variety of movements among a variety of American Indian peoples.

Of particular interest to sociologists have been the two Ghost Dance movements in the western United States, one about 1870 among Indian peoples in Nevada, California, and southern Oregon, and one about 1890 among Indian peoples over a very wide area of the western half of the United States. "Acculturation and Messianic Movements" [19], by Bernard Barber, is a speculative discussion of both Ghost Dance movements that posits sociocultural deprivation as the underlying cause of most messianic movements. Michael P. Carroll's "Revitalization Movements and Social Structure: Some Quantitative Tests" [51] is concerned only with the 1890 dance. Drawing from the work of Barber and others, Carroll "tests" various explanations of why not all tribes exposed to the Ghost Dance accepted its beliefs. The paper has generated some comment and discussion on its methodological shortcomings, and it has stimulated other short examinations of the acceptance of the 1890 Ghost Dance. One comment is offered by Kaye Brown in "Quantitative Testing and Revitalization Behavior: On Carroll's Explanation of the Ghost Dance" [46], and another has been offered by Gail Landsman in "The Ghost Dance and the Policy of Land Allotment" [160]. Also pertinent are Carroll's rejoinders to these comments [52, 53].

The Handsome Lake Movement among the Iroquois of New York is the subject of Anthony F. C. Wallace's "Handsome Lake and the Great Revival in the West" [302]. Wallace relates the Handsome Lake Movement to another religious movement—that of the Mormons—in the same place and period. The Handsome Lake Movement is also one of three examples discussed by Frank W. Young in his "Reactive Subsystems" [329], an analysis of groups in opposition to the larger systems within which they are located. The same movement is also one of three analyzed by Fred Voget in "The American Indian in Transition: Reformation and Status Innovations" [293], the other two being the Shakerism of the Pacific Northwest and the Peyotism of the Plains. Descriptions of religious ceremonies involved in movements are provided by Bernhard J. Stern for Shakerism in "An Indian Shaker Initiation and Healing Service" [265] and by John James Collins for Peyotism in "Transformations of the Self and the Duplication of Ceremonial Structure" [70].

Another revitalistic movement is discussed by Robert K. Thomas in "The Redbird Smith Movement" [270]. Occurring among the traditional Cherokees in the hills of northeastern Oklahoma at the turn of this century, the Redbird Smith movement was an effort to regain and preserve what the *Ketoowahs* (Cherokee People) had lost. It was somewhat unusual, since Redbird Smith was not really considered a prophet. The Cherokees do not allow a mere individual to initiate action or determine the fate of the group. In this sense it was not a messianic movement. Comments on Thomas's paper have been offered by Fred W. Voget [294].

Relations with Minority and Majority Groups

The area of sociology most applicable to the study of American Indians is minority relations. It is not surprising that this section is the largest in the bibliography despite our attempts to limit the number of entries. We have restricted it to publications that deal with minority relations per se, that is, with relations between individual members of minority groups (including ethnic groups), between these members and members of the majority group, or between the groups.

Individual Relations

The first literature to be discussed considers individual members of groups. One manner in which the subject of American Indian minority relations has been addressed on the individual level is through the causes and consequences of interaction. Such are the bases of Burt W. Aginsky's essay "The Interaction of Ethnic Groups: A Case Study of Indians and Whites" [8], which discusses the history of the ways Indians and Whites relate to one another. The effects of shared and divergent values on the interaction of Crees and

Whites are the theme of John J. Honigman's discussion, "Interpersonal Relations and Ideology in a Northern Canadian Community" [135]. Indian and White everyday interaction is discussed by Rosalie H. Wax and Robert K. Thomas in "American Indians and White People" [314]. Wax and Thomas pay particular attention to the normative bases of misunderstandings in this interaction. Also, Jean L. Briggs provides a personal description of her interaction with Eskimos in "Kapluna Daughter: Living with the Eskimos" [43].

Another way American Indian minority relations on the individual level may be approached is by examining individual attitudes, beliefs, and values. Five articles and one anthology on this topic were published in the middle 1970s. "Some Evidence of Canadian Ethnic, Racial, and Sexual Antagonism" [158], by Sanford Labovitz, is a research note reporting a study of prejudice toward Indians and French in midwestern Canada. Both "Monologues in Red and White: Contemporary Racial Attitudes in Two Southern Plains Communities" [240], by William W. Savage, Jr., and "The Perceived Structure of American Ethnic Groups: The Use of Multidimensional Scaling in Stereotype Research" [95], by Sandra G. Funk, Abraham D. Horowitz, Raanan Lipshitz, and Forrest W. Young, focus on the nature of stereotypes, using very different techniques. Savage uses oral histories in his comparison of Indian and White stereotypes among members of two rural Oklahoma communities, and Funk et al. examine the utility of multidimensional scaling in their study of stereotypes of American Indians and twelve other ethnic groups. A Canadian study of how the social class of ethnic groups (including American Indians) influences the attitudes of Whites toward these groups is reported in James S. Frideres's "Prejudice towards Minority Groups: Ethnicity or Class" [92]. In "Conservatism, Racial Intolerance, and Attitudes toward Racial Assimilation among Whites and American Indians" [15], Howard M. Bahr and Bruce A. Chadwick report a survey of Indians and Whites in Seattle and relate conservatism in the racial attitudes of the two groups. Henry Zentner's *The Indian Identity Crises* [330] is a collection of six papers primarily on Canadian Indians, most previously published, that discuss attitudes, values, aspirations, and identities of contemporary Indians and their relations with Whites.

Group Relations

The study of American Indians' relations with minority and majority groups on the group level encompasses a variety of topics, ranging from the history of such relations, to government policies, to assimilation. A series of four articles appeared in the *American Journal of Sociology* in 1929, 1930, 1931, and 1932 entitled "Race Relations." These assess the relations of Blacks and American Indians with the larger society. Three were written by Melville J. Herskovits [127, 128; 129] and one by T. J. Woofter, Jr. [326].

Four essays, two from the 1940s and two from the 1950s, describe the historical interrelations between American Indians and other ethnic groups. In "Role of the Indian in the Race Relations Complex of the South" [35], Leonard Bloom considers the role of Indians in three types of historical relationships in the southeastern United States: as slaves of Whites, as slaveholders of Blacks, and as part of the rise of mixed-blood (Black, White, and Indian) "racial islands." The historical contacts between Pueblo, Spanish, and Anglo groups in the Southwest are described by E. K. Francis in "Multiple Intergroup Relations in the Upper Rio Grande Region" [91]. Very broad descriptive overviews of early European-Indian contacts have been offered by Thomas F. McIlwraith for Canada in "The Indians of Canada" [174] and by D'Arcy McNickle for the United States in "Indian and European: Indian-White Relations from Discovery to 1887" [184].

Historical relations of American Indians and White religious groups have also been examined within sociology. Puritans and American Indians were discussed very early in the history of sociology in the United States by Louis Martin Sears in "The Puritan and His Indian Ward" [244] and very recently by Philip L. Berg in "Racism and the Puritan Mind" [23]. Beverly P. Smaby examines the conflicts between the ecological systems of early Mormons and American Indians in the Great Basin region of the United States in "The Mormons and the Indians" [251].

Two theoretical articles on minority relations are provided by Donald G. Baker. In "Color, Culture and Power: Indian-White Relations in Canada and America" [17], he analyzes three major historical bases for the development of racism toward American Indians. In "Identity, Power and Psychocultural Needs: White Responses to Non-whites" [18], Baker expands this analysis to include contemporary racism toward Blacks and Asian-Americans as well as toward American Indians.

More than any other minority group in the United States (and perhaps more than any other minority group in the world), American Indians have been the object of a variety of formal social policies and laws. These may be thought of as the outcome of the relationship between American Indians as a minority group and the White majority. Some of these policies and laws are (or were) unique to American Indians and define their special legal status in American society. Policies and laws that affect (or affected) minorities besides Indians usually revolve around the issue of assimilation.

For ease of presentation, we have divided the literature here into two groups: one that pertains to government administration and another that pertains to assimilation.

The literature on government administration of American Indians, though appearing within the publications of sociology, tends not to be very sociological in nature. It mostly describes what the federal government has done, does, or should do regarding the affairs of American Indians. This literature is useful in providing a perspective, particularly a historical one, of government-Indian relations, but it does not contribute greatly to the discipline of sociology.

Included within this literature are Francis E. Leupp's "Indian Lands: Their Administration with Reference to Present and Future Use" [164]; Arthur C. Parker's "The Social Elements of the Indian Problem" [215]; John Collier's "United States Indian Administration as a Laboratory of Ethnic Relations" [67]; and John Collier and Laura Thompson's "The Indian Education and Administration Research" [68]. Also included is "A New Image for the Great White Father" [202] by James E. Officer.

An entire 1957 issue of the *Annals of the American Academy of Political and Social Science* is devoted to American Indians. Entitled "American Indians and American Life" [250] and edited by George E. Simpson and J. Milton Yinger, the issue is a milestone in the social science study of American Indians and American Indian concerns. This work was updated in 1978 as "American Indians Today" [328]. Five of the articles in the 1957 issue contain discussions of the administration of Indian affairs: "The Legal Aspects of Indian Affairs from 1887 to 1957" [109], by Theodore H. Haas; "The Role of the Bureau of Indian Affairs since 1933" [331], by William Zimmerman, Jr.; "Termination of Federal Supervision: Disintegration and the American Indian" [159], by Oliver LaFarge; "Termination of Federal Supervision: The Removal of Restrictions over Indian Property and Person" [305], by Arthur V. Watkins; and "The Indian Claims Commission Act" [171], by Nancy Oestreich Lurie. Similar articles in the 1978 update are: "The Bureau of Indian Affairs: Activities since 1945" [49], by Raymond V. Butler; "The Bureau of Indian Affairs since 1945: An Assessment" [203], by James E. Officer; "Legislation and Litigation concerning American Indians" [72], by Vine Deloria, Jr.; and "The Indian Claims Commission" [172], by Nancy Oestreich Lurie.

There are also some relatively recent articles on Canadian government policies. They are J. Melling's "Recent Developments in Official Policy towards Canadian Indians and Eskimos" [192]; A. W. R. Carrothers's "Canada: Reluctant Imperialist" [54]; Robert

C. Fairfield's "New Towns in the Far North" [83]; R. W. Dunning's "The Indian Situation: A Canadian Government Dilemma" [82]; and L. F. S. Upton's "The Origins of Canadian Indian Policy" [292].

Solving "The Indian Problem": The White Man's Burdensome Business [310], edited by Murray L. Wax and Robert W. Buchanan, is a collection of essays and news stories drawn from the *New York Times* over the past hundred years. It is useful and informative and gives a good impression of how American Indian–White relations have been viewed (primarily) by Whites.

Concern with the assimilation of American Indians into larger American society was evident very early in sociological literature. In 1902 Sarah E. Simons devoted part of her paper "Social Assimilation" [249] to American Indians, describing how the United States promotes assimilation through education and suffrage.

In a series of articles published about 1930, "The Socialization of the American Indian" [32], "The Social Assimilation of the American Indian" [31], and "The American Indian and Status" [33], Frank Wilson Blackmar calls rather emphatically for the use of education to assimilate American Indians.

Around the middle of this century, the nature of the literature changed, and authors no longer called for the assimilation of American Indians. They began to treat assimilation as a sociological concept and to examine its implications.

Both the papers "Acculturation and Personality" [99], by John Gillin and Victor Raimy, and "The Measurement of Assimilation: The Spokane Indians" [236], by Prodipto Roy, are on the measurement of assimilation. The former is based on research among the Lac du Flambeau band of Chippewas in northern Wisconsin, and the latter is based on research among the Spokane Indians on the Spokane Reservation, Washington. A paper by Edward P. Dozier, George E. Simpson, and J. Milton Yinger, "The Integration of Americans of Indian Descent" [79], is an insightful treatment of differences between the concepts of assimilation and integration. It is argued that integration can be obtained without assimilation. An article with the same title by J. Milton Yinger and George Eaton Simpson [327] is found in the earlier-mentioned "American Indians Today" [328].

The implications of assimilation have been discussed in three papers we located within sociology. Evon Z. Vogt, in a paper entitled "The Acculturation of American Indians" [295], provides an overview of the degree of resistance to acculturation present within various Indian tribes. "On 'Americanizing' the American Indian" [147], a 1958 paper by Horace M. Kallen, contains a discussion of the national image of American Indians, "Americanism," and resulting assimilation policy problems. A more recent perspective on assimilation is presented in Albert L. Wahrhaftig and Robert K. Thomas's "Renaissance and Repression: The Oklahoma Cherokee" [299]. They discuss the political and economic consequences of perpetuating the myth of Cherokee assimilation in Oklahoma.

Other

There are five noteworthy book-length treatments placing sociological emphasis on American Indians as a minority group in the United States. The earliest is a social and historical examination published in 1928 by William Christie MacLeod. Entitled *The American Indian Frontier* [179], it is one of the first scholarly books pertaining to sociology and American Indians. *Native Americans Today: Sociological Perspectives* [16] is a reader published in 1972 and edited by Howard M. Bahr, Bruce A. Chadwick, and Robert C. Day. It contains forty-two papers, most published previously, that consider various "sociological" aspects of contemporary American Indians. A somewhat similar collection of readings published in the same year is *The Emergent Native Americans: A Reader in Culture Contact* [301], edited by Deward E. Walker, Jr.

Niels Winther Braroe's social psychological study *Indian and White: Self-Image and Interaction in a Canadian Plains Community* [42] emphasizes the self-concepts of the Crees resulting from their interactions with Whites.

In his well-known *Indian Americans: Unity and Diversity* [309], Murray L. Wax attempts to present a general picture of American Indians in terms of their history (particularly their history vis-à-vis "White" America), their contemporary communities, and their place in and relationship to the larger society. A significant portion of the book is drawn from Wax's research on the Cherokees in northeastern Oklahoma and, to a much lesser extent, the Pine Ridge Sioux.

American Indians and Social Stratification

The literature on social stratification and American Indians is heterogeneous. We have subdivided it into four rather general categories: the special legal status of American Indians in the United States and in

Canada; social and economic position of American Indians in the larger society; stratification within Indian societies; and mixed-blood communities.

Legal Status

In the previous section we briefly discussed works that provide some information about the special legal status of American Indians as a minority group. Here we present the sociological literature that deals extensively with this unique status and its implications.

In "An Indian Dilemma" [243], Ernest L. Schusky describes contradictions in the special legal relationship between Indians and the federal government. He details the dilemma of Indian individuals in often having to choose between their rights as members of tribes and the civil liberties accorded most citizens of the United States—for example, due process, education, and religious freedom. This dilemma is further illustrated in Warren Weston's "Freedom of Religion and the American Indian" [317].

The special legal status of Canadian Indians also has been discussed in the literature. In "The Dialectic of Indian Life in Canada" [86], A. D. Fisher outlines problems of the status relationship between reservation members and White administrators. In "Dakota Indian Ethnicity in Saskatchewan" [149], Alice B. Kehoe provides an overview of the legal status problems of the Dakota Indians that have resulted from the shifting policies of the Canadian government.

Social and Economic Position

A number of works have been published since the early 1960s that examine the position of Indians within the social and economic structure of the United States and Canada. Calvin F. Schmid and Charles E. Nobbe's "Socioeconomic Differentials among Non-white Races" [241] is an analysis of educational, income, and occupational data on five groups, including American Indians, for the period 1940 to 1960. Compared with Negroes, Japanese, Chinese, Whites, and a composite classification called "other," American Indians consistently ranked at or very near the bottom on all indicators over the entire period. In "The Effect of Education on the Earnings of Indian, Eskimo, Métis, and White Workers in the Mackenzie District of Northern Canada" [155], Chun-yan Kuo finds that education influences the later earnings of Indians more than those of the other groups.

The relationship of the social and economic class level of American Indians to other features of their life has also been researched. Harriet J. Kupferer looks at the significant effects of social and economic characteristics on the educational aspirations and health practices of North Carolina Cherokees in "Health Practices and Educational Aspirations as Indicators of Acculturation and Social Class among the Eastern Cherokee" [156]. Similarly, John P. Walter's "Two Poverties Equal Many Hungry Indians: An Economic and Social Study of Nutrition" [304] is an analysis of the relative influence of socioeconomic and attitudinal factors on the nutritional behavior of Paiute reservation youth.

Stratification within Indian Societies

The sociological literature also contains examinations of social stratification within historic and contemporary American Indian societies.

Several studies on this topic were published during the first four decades of this century. Two of these consider leadership. As a conclusion to a detailed discussion of the Australian Aborigines, Eben Mumford, in "Origins of Leadership, III" [198], gives an overview of leadership among North American tribes, comparing it with types found in Australia. Jessie Bernard stresses the psychological mechanisms underlying American Indian tribal leadership in her "Political Leadership among North American Indians" [24]. Bernard argues that leadership was based primarily on psychological, not institutional factors. She also makes the seemingly unfortunate statement that the behavior and qualities of this leadership were determined by the "nature of Indian human nature," whatever that might mean.

Historical American Indian societies are also featured in papers by Brewton Berry, William Christie MacLeod, and Ralph Linton. In a somewhat superficial study, "Democracy in Primitive Society" [25], Berry discusses differences between tribal stratification systems. MacLeod describes types of slavery found among tribes of the Northwest Coast in "Some Aspects of Primitive Chattel Slavery" [177]. Linton's "A Neglected Aspect of Social Organization" [165] is a very insightful treatment of age grades, sex differences, and the family systems of the traditional Comanches and the Tanalas of Madagascar.

Discussions of stratification within contemporary Indian societies are more recent, dating from the middle 1930s. The first of these is Mapheus Smith's study of student leaders at Haskell Institute, "A Comparative Study of Indian Student Leaders and Followers" [252]. A decade later Margaret Cussler published "Film-making as a Focus of Social Forces in an Indian Tribe" [71], a discussion of efforts at making a documentary film among the Hopis and of the internal tribal problems resulting from it.

Three papers have appeared on this subject in the past ten years. One, "Territory, Village Identity, and the Modern Eskimo Reindeer Manager" [204], by Dean F. Olson, is a good examination of the importance that territorial origins continue to have in defining social relations between the Eskimo herd owner and village members. The reindeer manager, according to Olson, must balance the owner's village relationships with those of the marketplace. Merwyn S. Garbarino's "Seminole Girl" [96] is a case history of the problems created by the "undefined status" of a young college-educated woman returning to her reservation. C. Thomas Brockman's "Correlation of Social Class and Education on the Flathead Indian Reservation, Montana" [44], reports that, in contrast with larger American society, there is no correlation between educational level and social class standing in the local class structure of the Flatheads in Montana.

Mixed-Blood Communities

Perhaps owing to the popularity of the concept of "marginal man" at the time, substantial sociological work on mixed-blood communities within the United States was done in the 1940s and 1950s. These part-Indian groups are typically found to have very marginal status and to be extremely isolated.

A general discussion of the history, population,

and institutions of one mixed group is found in Margaret Mary Wood's "The Russian Creoles of Alaska as a Marginal Group" [325]. Roland M. Harper and Guy B. Johnson have studied the Croatans of North and South Carolina, an Indian-White-Black enclave that has experienced a variety of social and legal status problems. Harper provides various demographic, social, and economic data in "A Statistical Study of the Croatans" [115]. Johnson, in "Personality in a White-Indian-Negro Community" [142], limits himself to the largest subdivision of this group, that of Robeson County, North Carolina, considering the effects that their unique status has on them.

Brewton Berry surveys the status problems of several triracial communities in South Carolina in "The Mestizos of South Carolina" [26]. He asserts that members of these groups, unlike those in other states, have been unwilling to assume the status of either Indian or Black but are unable to acquire the status of White. An interesting outline of the demographic, social organizational, and status characteristics of ten of the largest triracial groups in the eastern United States is provided by William Harlen Gilbert, Jr., in "Memorandum concerning the Characteristics of the Larger Mixed-Blood Racial Islands of the Eastern United States" [97]. Vernon J. Parenton and Roland J. Pellegrin present a good overview of the characteristics of another group in their "The 'Sabines': A Study of Racial Hybrids in a Louisiana Coastal Parish" [214]. The authors concentrate on the social, cultural, and racial isolation of these people. Finally, the "Brandywine" population of southern Maryland is studied in "Trends in Mate Selection in a Tri-racial Isolate" [118] by Thomas J. Harte. For further references to this issue see *Indians in Maryland and Delaware: A Critical Bibliography* [222], by Frank W. Porter, III, in this series.

Economies and Economic Concerns

Sociological publications on economics and the American Indian have followed very definite trends. Before 1940 the emphasis was decidedly on the economic characteristics of pre-Columbian and very early contact societies. After a fifteen-year hiatus of activity in this area, sociological considerations turned toward contemporary Indian economic systems and concerns.

Traditional Economies

The nature of traditional American Indian economic systems is addressed in Clark Wissler's article, "Aboriginal Maize Culture as a Typical Cultural-Complex" [322], describing aspects of maize production among different tribes. Traditional economies are also examined by E. B. Renaud in "Influence of Food on Indian Culture" [226], an analysis of the dependence of the Plains tribes on the buffalo. David G. Mandelbaum's "Boom Periods in the History of an Indian Tribe" [186] describes the effect of the horse, gun, and railroad on the economy of the Plains Crees. In "Big Business and the North American Indian" [180], by William Christie MacLeod, the laissez-faire attitudes of North Europeans toward Indians of the seventeenth century are compared with Spanish attempts at economic integration. "The Changing Character of Fox Adoption-Feasts" [194], by Truman Michelson, is an analysis of the adoption-feast as an institution fostering the exchange of economic goods within the tribe. It also describes changes that occurred as a result of European contact.

Contemporary Economies and Economic Issues

The earliest article we located dealing with contemporary economics is D. B. Shimkin's 1955 paper "The Economy of a Trapping Center: The Case of Fort Yukon, Alaska" [245]. Two years later, in "The Economic Basis of Indian Life" [150], William H. Kelly reported income and labor force characteristics, reservation resources and development programs, and tribal income and expenditure figures for American Indians throughout the United States.

The Navajos have been the subject of a variety of economic research. Two articles on the Navajos written by Tom T. Sasaki in the 1950s describe economic development projects on the Navajo Reservation in New Mexico. "Sociocultural Problems in Introducing New Technology on a Navaho Irrigation Project" [238] is a discussion of problems leading to the failure of a "model farm," and "Situational Changes and the Fruitland Navaho" [239] examines the effect of steady work on Navajos living near the Fruitland Irrigation Project. Two articles on economic development on the Navajo Reservation were published in 1976. Peter Iverson, in "Legal Assistance and Navajo Economic Revitalization" [139], discusses the economic and political successes occurring through the DNA, a legal aid agency for the Navajos that had been in operation for about ten years. Lorraine Turner Ruffing, in "Navajo Economic Development Subject to Cultural Restraints" [237], examines the reasons underlying the lack of more successful economic development among the Navajos. Based on her fieldwork, she recommends that federal planners adopt a new "model" for economic development that recognizes the social and cultural systems of the Navajos.

H. Clyde Wilson and Leo J. Wolfe use data from the Jicarilla Apache Reservation to test the belief of many Americans that individuals will not work if they are provided with unearned income sufficient to maintain their standard of living. Entitled "The Relationship between Unearned Income and Individual Productive Effort on the Jicarilla Apache Indian Reservation" [321], the report of their study shows that between 1947 and 1958 an increase in per capita tribal payments (i.e., unearned income) led to increased, not decreased sheep production.

The economic development of the Canadian North is the subject of two papers. In "The Coming Crisis in the North" [232], R. G. Robertson discusses the potential for development in general, noting "native adjustment" as a major problem to be faced. Paul Deprez, in "The Economic Development of the Canadian North: With or without the Indians?" [75], asserts that Canadian officials regard the Indians of northern Canada as "nonadaptable" compared with the Eskimos. He then argues that this fosters the mistaken attitude that urban relocation is the only solution for Canada's "Indian problem."

The results of a field study on the Wind River Reservation, Wyoming, investigating the development, operations, and sociocultural implications of the Arapaho Ranch (an economic enterprise of the Northern

Arapaho Tribe) are reported in "The Arapahoe Ranch: An Experiment in Cultural Change and Economic Development" [89], by Loretta Fowler.

Alan L. Sorkin's book *American Indians and Federal Aid* [255], a volume in the Brookings Studies in Social Economics, is a good, relatively recent (1971) statement and evaluation of federal government assistance programs for American Indians. It covers such topics as the Indian on the reservation, education, health, agricultural, industrial and manpower development, property and income management, and welfare services. Sorkin concludes with suggestions for improvement in these areas. Data pertaining to American Indians are presented throughout the book and in three appendices. Sorkin addresses similar issues in his paper "The Economic Basis of Indian Life" [257]. He also presents a variety of data on manufacturing enterprises on reservations over the past twenty years and discusses factors inhibiting further industrial development in "Business and Industrial Development on American Indian Reservations" [256].

Politics and Political Movements

Publications on American Indian politics and political movements cover the three general topics of pan-Indianism, self-determination, and participation in the political system of the United States.

Three articles consider pan-Indianism. Two offer rather general though informative descriptions of pan-Indianism since early European contact. These are "Pan-Indianism" [271], by Robert K. Thomas, and "Nationalistic Trends among American Indians" [323], by Shirley Hill Witt. Somewhat more analytical is "Intertribal Attitudes among Native American Youth" [84], by Joe R. Feagin and Randall Anderson. Using data obtained from students at a Bureau of Indian Affairs boarding school, the authors found fairly high tolerance among youth toward members of different tribes as well as toward Whites.

Although the Indian Reorganization Act of 1934 was a milestone in the history of Indian–federal government relationships, as well as the beginning of federal recognition on many issues of tribal self-determination, no sociological publication on self-determination appeared for twenty years after the act. The first such study was Robert W. Rietz's "Leadership, Initiative and Economic Progress on an American Indian Reservation" [230]. More important is Henry F. Dobyns's "Therapeutic Experience of Responsible Democracy" [77], an analysis of the administration of Indian peoples by the federal government since 1933, the year John Collier took office as commissioner of Indian affairs.

Events and activities on specific reservations have also been studied. Robert L. Bee's "Tribal Leadership in the War on Poverty: A Case Study" [21] is an analysis of the self-help programs of the tribal council on the Fort Yuma Reservation. In their paper "Community Control and the Reservation: Self-Interest as a Factor Limiting Reform" [47], William P. Browne and Michael Davis report a survey of leaders on the Isabella Reservation in Michigan. A most important paper is Ronald L. Trosper's case study "Native American Boundary Maintenance: The Flathead Indian Reservation, Montana, 1860–1970" [285]. It is a solid analysis of changing "definitions of Indian" by one Indian tribe and of their adoption of a racial definition based on blood quantum in an attempt to preserve themselves as a distinct social and cultural group.

Finally, there are several articles on the political activities of American Indians. The first is John Collier's rather laudatory discussion of the involvement of American Indians in America's World War II effort, "The Indian in a Wartime Nation" [66]. More interesting is Helen L. Peterson's "American Indian Political Participation" [217], which covers both the history and the contemporary involvement of Indians in American political life. A case study of the involvement of American Indians in local political life is provided by Ronald L. Neff and Jay A. Weinstein in "Iowa's Indians Come of Age" [201]. Political views of and about American Indians are reported by Leonard G. Ritt in "Some Social and Political Views of American Indians" [231] and by Robert Panzarella and Ansley LaMar in "Attitudes of Blacks and Whites toward Native American Revolutionary Tactics for Social Change" [213].

Social Control and Judicial Systems

We have grouped publications on social control and judicial systems into three categories: traditional tribal control; American Indians and criminal justice systems; and social disorganization and criminal behavior. Most of the publications in this area appearing before the early 1940s were on traditional methods of social control; most since then are on the other two topics.

Traditional Tribal Control

The *Journal of Criminal Law and Criminology* (formerly the *Journal of the American Institute of Criminal Law and Criminology*) published most early articles on traditional methods of social control. This includes three articles written by William Christie MacLeod in the 1930s. "Aspects of the Earlier Development of Law and Punishment" [181] is an overview of various legal customs primarily of Northwest Coast tribes; "Law, Procedure, and Punishment in Early Bureaucracies" [182] is a description of traditional methods of handling deviants, mostly within eastern woodland and southeastern tribes, for example, Hurons and Menominees, Creeks and Choctaws; and "Police and Punishment among Native Americans of the Plains" [183] is a discussion of methods of social control, particularly the use of police societies, by the Cheyennes, Crows, Ojibwas, and Sioux. These Plains tribes and their police societies were also the focus of Norman D. Humphrey's 1942 article in the *Journal of Criminal Law and Criminology*, "Police and Tribal Welfare in Plains Indian Culture" [138].

E. Adamson Hoebel provides a much broader overview of social control in "Law-ways of the Primitive Eskimos" [133]. He discusses leadership, property norms, and legal homicide as well as criminal homicide and sorcery in traditional Eskimo societies. A. I. Hallowell looks at only one mechanism of social control in his "The Social Function of Anxiety in a Primitive Society" [113]. Focusing on the beliefs and practices of the Lake Winnipeg Salteaux Ojibwa tribe regarding disease, Hallowell discusses the role of anxiety in eliciting appropriate social behavior.

American Indians and Criminal Justice Systems

We have grouped a large number of papers under the subheading of criminal justice systems, all of which seem to relate in one manner or another to contemporary systems. Two papers from the 1920s by William Renwick Riddell were the earliest we discovered on issues regarding American Indians in the legal system of larger American society. His "The Sad Tale of an Indian Wife" [228] and "The Administration of Criminal Law in the Far North of Canada" [229] are both descriptions of cases involving natives in the Canadian criminal justice system.

It was not until the 1940s that articles on this topic again appeared. "The Delinquency of the American Indian" [296], by Hans von Hentig, reports statistics concerning arrests, sentences, and the nature of offenses for Indians in the 1930s and early 1940s. In "Variability in the Criminal Behavior of American Indians" [123], Norman S. Hayner discusses correlates of the prevalence of crime in various Indian communities, most of them in the Pacific Northwest.

Published in the 1960s was Donald E. Pettit's "A Study of Aspiration among Three Cultural Groups of Prisoners" [219]. This article compares the perceived present and future happiness of incarcerated Indians, Métis, and Whites. A description of a contemporary tribal judicial system by John James Collins entitled "Law Function and Judicial Process at a New Mexico Pueblo" [69] appeared in the late 1960s.

Since the early 1970s, there have been a relatively large number of articles on American Indians in the criminal justice systems of Canada and the United States.

Many Canadian publications on this topic have appeared in the *Canadian Journal of Criminology and Corrections*. That natives are disproportionately defendents in the Canadian criminal justice system is illustrated by Rita M. Bienvenue and A. H. Latif in "Arrest, Disposition and Recidivism: A Comparison of Indians and Whites" [29]. The authors analyze records of Winnipeg's criminal justice system to assess the extent to which Indian and White crime statistics reflect the population proportions of the two groups. They find that Indians are overrepresented in arrests, convictions, and all types of court dispositions, but not in recidivism. Specific factors unique to natives that explain this overrepresentation are examined in two articles. William T. Badcock outlines several problems caused by misunderstandings during interactions of natives with White representatives of the judicial system in "Problems of Native Offenders in the Correctional System" [13]. An attempt to provide legal assistance to overcome problems resulting in overrepresentation in the judicial system is described in "The Indian Counsellor Project—Help for the Accused" [22], by Michael C. Bennett. In "Violence among the Eskimos" [141], C. H. S. Jayewardene challenges the commonly held assumption that there is a relationship between Eskimos' alcohol consumption and violent behavior. In "An Assessment of Legal and Cultural Stigma regarding Unskilled Workers" [211], Theodore S. Palys reports an experiment to determine whether Indians and

Whites with similar criminal backgrounds experience significantly different employment opportunities.

In the United States, the journal *Criminology* contains two articles based on research in the Wind River Reservation, Wyoming area: "A Self-Report Comparison of Indian and Anglo Delinquency in Wyoming" [87], by Morris A. Forslund and Virginia A. Cranston, and "Delinquency among Wind River Reservation Youth" [88], by Morris A. Forslund and Ralph E. Meyers. In 1975 this same journal published a report of research conducted by Edwin L. Hall and Albert A. Simkus entitled "Inequality in the Types of Sentences Received by Native Americans and Whites" [112]. The findings are that American Indians are more likely than Whites to receive prison sentences.

Social Disorganization and Criminal Behavior

There have been several articles on aspects of "social disorganization" within Indian communities and how they may relate to criminal behavior. Mhyra S. Minnis published two papers based on field research on the Shoshone-Bannock tribes conducted at the Fort Hall Indian Reservation in Idaho: "Selected Social Problems of Fort Hall Reservation" [195] and "The Relationship of the Social Structure of an Indian Community to Adult and Juvenile Delinquency" [196]. In "Patterns of Illegitimacy on a Canadian Indian Reserve: 1860–1960" [37], Philip K. Bock examines the relationship between the rate of illegitimate births and the degree of social and cultural integration in a Canadian Indian community over a one-hundred-year period. Based on extensive ethnographic research in the Canadian Arctic and subarctic, John J. Honigmann and Irma Honigmann published "How Baffin Island Eskimos Have Learned to Use Alcohol" [137], and John J. Honigmann published "Social Disintegration in Five Northern Canadian Communities" [136]. American Indians in a Wisconsin community are one of three examples used by Arthur Lewis Wood in "Minority-Group Criminality and Cultural Integration" [324].

The American Indian Family

Sociologists have long been interested in the American Indian family. Unfortunately this interest has not been extensive, nor has it yielded a particularly large number of publications. We have classified the publications that do exist in this area into three subtopics: general considerations of family and kinship; child care and socialization; and sex roles.

General Considerations

The earliest general study of family and kinship within the broad sociological literature is Robert H. Lowie's 1914 paper "Social Organization" [166]. It is a critique of several anthropological theories of the evolution and functions of kinship forms (clans, gens, etc.) using examples from traditional native American societies. Traditional Northwest Coast tribes, for example, the Yuroks, Karoks, Hupas, and Kwakiutls, are the focus of William Christie MacLeod's description of the nature of marriage, divorce, and illegitimacy within a culture stressing economics in most aspects of social life. See his "Marriage, Divorce and Illegitimacy in a Primitive Pecuniary Culture" [178].

Burt W. Aginsky reports some reflections by an elderly Pomo man on the importance of the family in traditional Indian societies as compared with European societies. It has the intriguing title: "An Indian's Soliloquy" [7]. J. R. Fox analyzes contemporary functions of the Pueblo clan system of Cochiti Pueblo, New Mexico, in his case study "Therapeutic Rituals and Social Structure in Cochiti Pueblo" [90]. Albert Heinrich's "Divorce as an Integrative Social Factor among Eskimos" [125] is an interesting analysis of the functions of Eskimo kinship systems. A particularly interesting finding is that divorce and remarriage, like many other Eskimo practices, increase social integration by maximizing the number of relationships within Eskimo groups. It is a good example of how the study of native cultures may provoke a reexamination of a researcher's own preconceptions of a particular phenomenon.

Child Care and Socialization

We have placed five articles and one book within the category of child care and socialization. The earliest article, "Child Training in an Indian Tribe" [290], by Ruth M. Underhill, is a simple, short description of the parent-children interaction the author witnessed during a visit with a Papago family. The most recent article, "Ecology, Socialization, and Personality Development among Athabascans" [41], by L. Bryce Boyer, Ruth M. Boyer and Arthur E. Hippler, discusses Athabascan socialization techniques and is based on experiences with Chiricahua, Lipan, and Mescalero Apaches in New Mexico and with Tanaina and Upper Tanana in Alaska. In the middle 1950s, Thomas Rhys

Williams expanded on Underhill's short essay and delineated six major structural features of Papago socialization (e.g., reward and punishment, deference patterns) in "The Structure of the Socialization Process in Papago Society" [319]. About the same time, Stephen T. Boggs reported in "An Interactional Study of Ojibwa Socialization" [40] that changes in Ojibwa socialization patterns occurring in three communities in Wisconsin and Manitoba reflected trends in the larger society. Marvin K. Opler examines the "infant determinism" hypothesis (that children are molded in terms of their culture) in the light of evidence from southwestern tribes and other groups in "The Influence of Ethnic and Class Subcultures on Child Care" [206]. Ann H. Beuf's *Red Children in White America* [28] is a sensitive and scholarly examination of Indian children's racial attitudes and how they develop.

Sex Roles

A variety of publications consider the sex roles of American Indians, particularly those of women. North American Indian examples are used by Marvin K. Opler in "Women's Social Status and the Forms of Marriage" [205], a discussion of the relationship between female sex roles, social status, and society's rules governing marital and extramarital relationships. An interesting experimental study of decision influence between husbands and wives from three social groups—Navajos, Mormons, and Texas farmers—is reported by Fred L. Strodtbeck in "Husband-Wife Interaction over Revealed Differences" [266]. Three papers focus on how sex roles may change in response to external influences. In "A Resultant of Intercultural Relations" [9], Burt W. Aginsky and Ethel G. Aginsky describe the influence of "White" culture in changing the Pomo from a male-dominated society to one that is female-dominated. Kendall Blanchard, in "Changing Sex Roles and Protestantism among Navajo Women in Ramah" [34], analyzes the involvement of Navajo women in the Protestant missions of Ramah, New Mexico, as a correlate of their changing sex roles. Ann Metcalf, in "From Schoolgirl to Mother: The Effects of Education on Navajo Women" [193], also examines the roles of Navajo women but focuses on the effect that attending federally-sponsored boarding schools has on adult self-esteem and maternal attitudes.

American Indian Education

Sociological interest in the education of American Indians is, with few exceptions, recent and not extensive. Of the sixteen works we have identified, only five were published before 1960, despite the fact that American Indian education has been a major policy objective of both governmental and religious organizations for several hundred years. This neglect is even more surprising when one considers that three of the earliest colleges established in this country—Harvard (1636), William and Mary (1693), and Dartmouth (1769)—were expressly charged with the responsibility of educating Indian youth.

The earliest work included in this bibliography that considers the education of American Indians was published in 1892. Frank Wilson Blackmar's polemical essay "Indian Education" [30] stresses the importance of education as a means to "civilize" American Indians and enumerates various problems encountered in such efforts. The next paper in the sociology of American Indian education appeared fifty years later — "Education, Child-Training, and Culture" [191], by Scudder Mekeel. The author examines certain basic assumptions of past attempts at educating American Indians, then suggests some new strategies that may more successfully impose American society and culture on American Indian youth. A decade later, Charles F. Jones published his "Notes on Indian Education" [144], a report of two problems in the attempted education of Papago youth. The first of these problems was a geographical one encompassing distance from school and family migration around and out of the reservation. The second problem was cultural in nature, involving the importance of the group as opposed to the individual and of cooperation as opposed to competition.

Two articles in the 1957 special volume of the *Annals of the American Academy of Political and Social Science* on the American Indian are concerned with education. In "Education among American Indians: Institutional Aspects" [275], Hildegard Thompson reviews the history and institutional nature of Indian education, including the mission and federal schools, major policy decisions, and public school education. Robert J. Havighurst, in "Education among American Indians: Individual and Cultural Aspects" [119], discusses cultural conflicts and individual motivation, intelligence, and achievement. In the 1978 special volume of the *Annals,* Havighurst discusses recent developments in the education of American Indians in his paper "Indian Education since 1960" [120].

W. W. Ludeman offers a cursory statistical summary of the college careers of Indian students at a South Dakota state teachers college in "The Indian Student in College" [170]. Robert V. Dumont, Jr. and Murray L. Wax write on "Cherokee School Society and the Intercultural Classroom" [81]. James G. Anderson and Dwight Safar study how community and school personnel's perception of Anglo, Spanish American, and Indian students' abilities influences provision of equal educational opportunities in their paper "The Influence of Differential Community Perceptions on the Provision of Equal Educational Opportunities" [12]. Their findings indicate that Spanish American and Indian children are viewed as less capable than Anglo children and that the children internalize this view.

Canadian Eskimo education is the topic of two very good articles by Charles W. Hobart. The first, "Eskimo Education, Danish and Canadian: A Comparison" [132], coauthored with C. S. Brant, compares the relative effectiveness of the Danish system of education in Greenland and the Canadian system in the Canadian Arctic. The Danish system, it is argued, emphasizes "cultural continuity," and very recently "cultural synthesis," while the Canadian system emphasizes "cultural replacement." Marked differences in both personal and cultural integrity are found to result from the different emphases. The second article, "Eskimo Education in the Canadian Arctic" [131], considers teacher effectiveness with Indian and Eskimo children. The study finds that Eskimo teachers, even if poorly trained, are more effective than White teachers in the early grades.

Canadian natives are also the subject of A. D.

Fisher's "White Rites vs. Indian Rites" [85] and Rodney A. Clifton's research note "The Social Adjustment of Native Students in a Northern Canadian Hostel" [59]. The former is an essay on the relevance of the expanded educational opportunities for Canadian Indians. The conclusion is that the "rituals" of White education often conflict with the value systems of Indians. The research note reports a study of Indian, Eskimo, and Métis students in a religious boarding school in the Northwest Territories of Canada.

We located three publications on education and sociology from the extensive research on the educational system of the Pine Ridge Reservation, South Dakota, by Murray and Rosalie Wax and others. A comprehensive report of this research is contained in the *Social Problems* publication "Formal Education in an American Indian Community" [312], by Murray L. Wax, Rosalie H. Wax, and Robert V. Dumont, Jr. "Indian Education for What?" [315], by Rosalie H. Wax and Murray L. Wax, is an interesting essay questioning whether the educational system really serves the needs of Indian youth. Rosalie Wax's "The Warrior Dropouts" [313] discusses reasons for the high attrition rate of Sioux males in the Pine Ridge High School. According to the author, many who fail to complete their schooling are really "pushouts" or "kickouts" rather than "dropouts."

To Live on This Earth: American Indian Education [94], by Estelle Fuchs and Robert J. Havighurst, is a good study of almost every facet of American Indian education. It emphasizes how Indian education varies throughout the United States. Much of the book is drawn from the authors' 1971 National Study of American Indian Education, done under the auspices of the United States Office of Education.

"Open School vs. Traditional School: Self-Identification among Native American and White Adolescents" [62], by William C. Cockerham and Audie L. Blevins, Jr., is an examination of the self-concepts of native American and White junior high school students on Wind River Reservation, Wyoming. The study relates these self-concepts to attendance at open and traditional schools. The authors find that open school Indian students had a more positive self-identification than traditional-school students, either Indian or White. The logical and theoretical structure underlying the study and the interpretation of findings has, however, been sharply criticized by Russell Thornton and Joan Marsh-Thornton [283]. Cockerham and Blevins have offered a rejoinder to this criticism [63].

Social Psychology of American Indians

Social-psychological studies of American Indians represent a relatively small part of the literature of sociology on American Indians. The topics most frequently discussed are personality traits, self-concepts, and anomie. A more extensive literature on the social psychology of American Indians may be found on the "boundary" between sociology and psychology, much of it published in the *Journal of Social Psychology*. The most common types of studies in this literature pertain to the intelligence and personality "testing" of American Indians. We have not included this literature because it is more psychological than sociological.

With the exception of John Gillin's "Personality in

Preliterate Societies" [98], a fairly extensive review of the literature pertaining primarily to personality studies in native North American societies, the early articles on social psychology of American Indians concern "modal" personality traits. "Personality Formation among the Navaho Indians" [153], by Clyde Kluckhohn, is a discussion of the relative influence of situational and cultural variables on personality formation. Anthony F. C. Wallace seriously questions the viability of the concept of "modal personality" in his research note "Individual Differences and Cultural Uniformities" [303]. He uses data from research on the Tuscarora Reservation in New York State to argue that culture has at most a probabilistic, not a deterministic effect on personality formation. "A Note on an Apparent Relationship between Tempermental Traits and Personality Traits" [140] is a study of the modal personalities of the Zuñis, Kwakiutls, and Dobus published in 1949 by Robert W. Janes. In 1957 two leaders in the study of American Indian personality, George D. Spindler and Louise S. Spindler, published "American Indian Personality Types and Their Sociocultural Roots" [260], an analysis of basic personality types within American Indian societies as manifestations of core psychological features.

American Indian and White Children: A Sociopsychological Investigation [121], by Robert J. Havighurst and Bernice L. Neugarten, reports studies of the moral and emotional development of Indian children and of the formulation of "tests" whereby this development may be studied. These studies were part of the massive research effort of the Indian Education Research Project of the Committee on Human Development of the

University of Chicago and the United States Office of Indian Affairs. Various other well-known publications resulted from this project, including *Warriors without Weapons: A Study of the Pine Ridge Sioux* [173], by Gordon Macgregor; *The Hopi Way* [276], by Laura Thompson and Alice Joseph; and *The Navaho* [163], by Dorothea C. Leighton and Clyde Kluckhohn.

Three articles from the late 1950s consider the effect of social stress on American Indian children. Alan C. Kerchoff and Thomas C. McCormick's "Marginal Status and Marginal Personality" [152] examines the relationship between marginal status characteristics and marginal personality traits among Ojibwa and White schoolchildren in northern Wisconsin. These same children were the subjects of Alan C. Kerchoff's "Anomie and Achievement Motivation: A Study of Personality Development within Cultural Disorganization" [151]. Theron Alexander and Robert Anderson studied stress among Northern Cheyenne children in "Children in a Society under Stress" [10]. They found that the general state of "stress" resulting from changes in Cheyenne society was reflected in the perceptions of the children.

The Navajo were one of four groups studied in Charles E. Osgood's report "The Cross-Cultural Generality of Visual-Verbal Synesthetic Tendencies" [208]. The other three groups were Whites, Japanese, and Mexican Americans. The Navajos, along with the Zuñis and Hopis, were also the subjects of Howard Maclay and Edward E. Ware's "Cross-Cultural Use of the Semantic Differential" [176].

Fieldwork among the Shoshones, Northern Arapahoes, and Whites on and around Wind River Reservation, Wyoming, was the basis for two articles by

Stanton K. Tefft. His "Anomy, Values, and Culture Change among Teen-age Indians: An Exploratory Study" [268] compares value commitments and anomic tendencies of these groups. His "Task Experience and Intertribal Value Differences on the Wind River Reservation" [269] discusses adults as well as youths and analyzes the individualistic/collectivistic and achievement orientations of the Shoshones and Northern Arapahoes. Both articles are valuable in illustrating the contrasts that may exist between two contemporary Indian peoples, even though they are geographically close.

Canadian Indian children are the subject of three papers published during the 1970s. Eleven-year-old boys from five Canadian ethnic groups, including Indians, are subjects for Kevin Marjoribanks's "Ethnic and Environmental Influences on Mental Abilities" [189]. The responses of young Indian and White children to Indian and White dolls are compared in "Racial and Cultural Identification among Canadian Indian Children" [105], by Carl F. Grindstaff, Wilda Galloway, and Joanne Nixon. Their work is patterned after Kenneth Clark's classic study of racial identification among Black children. A comparison of Cree and non-Indian junior high school students' self-concepts and school-related attitudes is found in Rodney A. Clifton's "Self-Concept and Attitudes: A Comparison of Canadian Indian and Non-Indian Students" [60].

Urbanization of American Indians

Sociological publications on American Indians in urban areas did not appear before the middle 1960s because American Indian populations in urban areas were small and not highly visible until about that time. Since then, American Indians have migrated to urban areas of the United States in large numbers. Generally this migration is to cities such as Los Angeles, San Francisco, Seattle, Minneapolis, Oklahoma City, Tulsa, and Phoenix, all of which are in states with large Indian populations, but it is also to major cities in states without significant Indian populations—for example, Chicago.

In the 1950s the Bureau of Indian Affairs (BIA) began an intensive program of urban relocation of American Indians. Although the program has not been responsible for all Indian migration to urban areas, this effort is certainly a major reason for this urbanization.

Several articles address the Bureau of Indian Affairs relocation programs. Joan Ablon's "American Indian Relocation: Problems of Dependency and Management in the City" [2] is one of the first considerations of urban Indians. It gives an overview of the nature of problems relating to employment, cultural maintenance, and family organization that BIA-sponsored relocatees to urban areas must confront. Alan L. Sorkin, in "Some Aspects of American Indian Migration" [254], analyzes data from a BIA-sponsored survey of participants in relocation programs. He examines education, earnings, and "antisocial" behavior and provides a broad overview of the success of the programs. Data from BIA-sponsored research have also been used by Lawrence Clinton, Bruce A. Chadwick, and Howard M. Bahr and are reported in their "Urban Relocation Reconsidered: Antecedents of Employment among Indian Males" [61]. Braxton M. Alfred takes a somewhat unusual approach in studying

BIA relocatees in "Blood Pressure Changes among Male Navaho Migrants to an Urban Environment" [11]. A recent evaluation of the BIA relocation program may be found in "Native American Indian Migration and Relocation: Success or Failure" [108], by James H. Gundlach and Alden E. Roberts.

Migration to urban areas not sponsored by BIA is discussed in Ruth Blumenfled's "Mohawks: Round Trip to the High Steel" [36]. She describes a migratory pattern of the Mohawk movement to New York City when employment in high steel construction is available and return "home" to the reservation during unemployment. A recent, broad discussion of American Indians in urban areas is provided by Sol Tax in "The Impact of Urbanization on American Indians" [267].

There are several comparative studies of Indians and other migrant groups in urban areas. Joan Ablon suggests that the characteristics American Indians bring to urban environment inhibit their successful adaptation in her comparative study "Retention of Cultural Values and Differential Urban Adaptation: Samoans and American Indians in a West Coast City" [3]. Arthur Margon, however, maintains that the Indian experience has not been very different from the experiences of other immigrant groups. In his paper "Indians and Immigrants: A Comparison of Groups New to the City" [188] he asserts that the problems of urban Indians should be traced to the nature of the urban situation rather than to unique cultural characteristics of American Indians.

Two papers coauthored by Bruce A. Chadwick discuss the adaptation of Indians to urban areas. In "Correlates of Length of Urban Residence among the

Spokane Indians" [57], Chadwick and Lynn C. White report the results of interviews with one hundred adult Spokane Indians, and in "The Assimilation of American Indians into Urban Society: The Seattle Case" [55] Chadwick and Joseph H. Strauss present data from Indians and Whites indicating the overall low assimilation of Indians in Seattle and showing no relationship between assimilation and length of time in the city.

Other relevant articles are "Correlates of Adjustment among American Indians in an Urban Environment" [190], by Harry W. Martin; "The Urbanization of the Yankton Indians" [117], by Wesley R. Hart, Jr.; "Alternative Models for the Study of Urban Migration" [103], by Theodore D. Graves; "Values, Expectations and Relocation: The Navaho Migrant to Denver" [104], by Theodore D. Graves and Minor Van Arsdale; and "Relocated American Indians in the San Francisco Bay Area: Social Interactions and Indian Identity" [1], by Joan Ablon.

Many of the problems experienced by urban Indians have been traced to inadequate relationships with urban institutions. In "Indian Powerlessness in Minnesota" [316], Joseph J. Westermeyer describes how Minnesota Indians are "powerless" within educational, health care, economic, and social service institutions in Minnesota cities and other locations. The inadequacies of social service agencies in serving natives in Anchorage, Alaska, have been discussed by Dorothy M. Jones in "The Mystique of Expertise in Social Services: An Alaskan Example" [145] and in "Interagency Conflict, Power, and Sanctioning Systems: An Alaskan Example" [146]. Bruce A. Chadwick, Joseph Strauss, Howard M. Bahr, and Lowell K. Halverson have published results of a survey on services available to Indians in dealing with criminal and civil legal problems in "Confrontation with the Law: The Case of the American Indians in Seattle" [56]. Fay G. Cohen's paper "The Indian Patrol in Minneapolis: Social Control and Social Change in an Urban Context" [64] describes a citizens' patrol organized for the purpose of averting potential legal problems in an Indian neighborhood.

Pan-Indianism as a stabilizing element in the adaptation of American Indians to urban environments is discussed by John A. Price in "The Migration and Adaptation of American Indians to Los Angeles" [223].

Trevor Denton has written two articles on the urbanization of Canadian Indians. In "Migration from a Canadian Indian Reserve" [73] he reports the results of fieldwork on a reserve and in a nearby city. His purpose was to discover the motivations for migration, adjustment to the urban area, and return to the reserve. In "Canadian Indian Migrants and Impression Management of Ethnic Stigma" [74] he presents the results of participant observation of a small group of Indian migrants to a city. He finds that some of the subjects disavow an "Indian identification," and he consequently examines their techniques of doing so.

There have been three books on the urbanization of American Indians. Jack O. Waddell and O. Michael Watson edited *The American Indian in Urban Society* [297], a collection of readings by anthropologists considering aspects of American Indian life in an urban environment. *Urban Renegades: The Cultural Strategy of American Indians* [106], by Jeanne Guillemin, is a case study of the Micmac in Boston. Alan L. Sorkin's *The*

Urban American Indian [258] is a very recent (1978) presentation of the social and economic characteristics of American Indians living in urban areas in the United States.

ALPHABETICAL LIST AND INDEX

* Denotes items suitable for secondary school students

Item no.		Essay page no.
[1]	Ablon, Joan. 1964. "Relocated American Indians in the San Francisco Bay Area: Social Interactions and Indian Identity." *Human Organization* 23:296–304.	(62)
[2]	———. 1965. "American Indian Relocation: Problems of Dependency and Management in the City." *Phylon* 26:362–71.	(60)
[3]	———. 1971. "Retention of Cultural Values and Differential Urban Adaptation: Samoans and American Indians in a West Coast City." *Social Forces* 49:385–92.	(61)
[4]	Abrahamson, Mark. 1969. "Correlates of Political Complexity." *American Sociological Review* 34:690–701.	(9)
[5]	Adair, John, Kurt Deuschle, and Walsh McDermott. 1957. "Patterns of Health and Disease among the Navahos." *Annals of the American Academy of Political and Social Science* 311:80–94.	(13)

[6]   Aginsky, Burt W. 1939. "Population Control in the Shanel (Pomo) Tribe." *American Sociological Review* 4:209–16.   (10)

[7]   ———. 1940. "An Indian's Soliloquy." *American Journal of Sociology* 46:43–44.   (50)

[8]   ———. 1949. "The Interaction of Ethnic Groups: A Case Study of Indians and Whites." *American Sociological Review* 14:288–93.   (25)

[9]   Aginsky, Burt W., and Ethel G. Aginsky. 1947. "A Resultant of Intercultural Relations." *Social Forces* 26:84–87.   (52)

[10]   Alexander, Theron, and Robert Anderson. 1957. "Children in a Society under Stress." *Behavioral Science* 2:46–55.   (58)

[11]   Alfred, Braxton M. 1970. "Blood Pressure Changes among Male Navaho Migrants to an Urban Environment." *Canadian Review of Sociology and Anthropology* 7:189–200.   (61)

[12]   Anderson, James G., and Dwight Safar. 1967. "The Influence of Differential Community Perceptions on the Provi-

sion of Equal Educational Opportunities." *Sociology of Education* 40:219–30.   (54)

[13]   Badcock, William T. 1976. "Problems of Native Offenders in the Correctional System." *Canadian Journal of Criminology and Corrections* 18:281–89.   (47)

[14]   Bahr, Howard M., and Brucc A. Chadwick. 1972. "Contemporary Perspectives on Indian Americans: A Review Essay." *Social Science Quarterly* 53:606–18.   (4)

[15]   ———. 1974. "Conservatism. Racial Intolerance, and Attitudes toward Racial Assimilation among Whites and American Indians." *Journal of Social Psychology* 94:45–56.   (26)

*[16]   Bahr, Howard M., Bruce A. Chadwick, and Robert C. Day, eds. 1972. *Native Americans Today: Sociological Perspectives.* New York: Harper and Row.   (33)

[17]   Baker, Donald G. 1972. "Color, Culture and Power: Indian-White Relations in Canada and America." *Canadian Review of American Studies* 3:3–20.   (28)

[18]   ———. 1974. "Identity, Power and Psychocultural Needs: White Responses

to Non-whites." *Journal of Ethnic Studies*
1:16–44.   (28)

[19]   Barber, Bernard. 1941. "Acculturation
and Messianic Movements." *American
Sociological Review* 6:663–69.   (23)

[20]   Barnett, H. G. 1941. "Personal
Conflicts and Cultural Change." *Social
Forces* 20:160–71.   (18)

[21]   Bee, Robert L. 1969. "Tribal Leadership in the War on Proverty: A Case
Study." *Social Science Quarterly* 50:676–
86.   (43)

[22]   Bennett, Michael C. 1973. "The Indian
Counsellor Project Help for the Accused." *Canadian Journal of Criminology
and Corrections* 15:1–6.   (47)

[23]   Berg, Philip L. 1975. "Racism and the
Puritan Mind." *Phylon* 36:1–7.   (28)

[24]   Bernard, Jessie. 1928. "Political Leadership among North American In-
dians." *American Journal of Sociology*
34:296–315.   (36)

[25]   Berry, Brewton. 1937. "Democracy in
Primitive Society." *Social Science*
12:96–101.   (36)

[26]   ———. 1945. "The Mestizos of South
Carolina." *American Journal of Sociology*
51:34–41.   (38)

[27]   ———. 1960. "The Myth of the Vanish-
ing Indian." *Phylon* 21:51–57.   (11)

[28]   Beuf, Ann H. 1977. *Red Children in
White America*. Philadelphia: University
of Pennsylvania Press.   (51)

[29]   Bienvenue, Rita M., and A. H. Latif.
1974. "Arrests, Disposition and Recidivism: A Comparison of Indians and
Whites." *Canadian Journal of Criminology
and Corrections* 16:105–16.   (47)

[30]   Blackmar, Frank Wilson. 1892. "Indian
Education." *Annals of the American
Academy of Political and Social Science*
2:813–37.   (52)

[31]   ———. 1929. "The Social Assimilation
of the American Indian." *Journal of
Educational Sociology* 3:7–19.   (31)

[32]   ———. 1929. "The Socialization of the
American Indian." *American Journal of
Sociology* 34:653–69.   (31)

[33]   ———. 1930. "The American Indian
and Status." *Sociology and Social Research*
14:221–32.   (31)

[34]   Blanchard, Kendall. 1975. "Changing Sex Roles and Protestantism among Navajo Women in Ramah." *Journal for the Scientific Study of Religion* 14:43–50.   (52)

[35]   Bloom, Leonard. 1940. "Role of the Indian in the Race Relations Complex of the South." *Social Forces* 19:268–73.   (27)

*[36]   Blumenfeld, Ruth. 1965. "Mohawks: Round Trip to the High Steel." *Transaction* 3:19–22.   (61)

[37]   Bock, Philip K. 1960. "Patterns of Illegitimacy on a Canadian Indian Reserve: 1860–1960." *Journal of Marriage and the Family* 26:142–48.   (48)

[38]   Bogardus, Emory S. 1952. "Symbolism in Totem Poles." *Sociology and Social Research* 36:247–51.   (17)

[39]   ———. 1957. "Social Life of the Cliff Dwellers." *Sociology and Social Research* 41:214–21.   (17)

[40]   Boggs, Stephen T. 1956. "An Interactional Study of Ojibwa Socialization." *American Sociological Review* 21:191–98.   (51)

[41]   Boyer, L. Bryce, Ruth M. Boyer, and Arthur E. Hippler. 1974. "Ecology, Socialization, and Personality Develop-

ment among Athabascans." *Journal of
Comparative Family Studies* 5:61–73.   (50)

[42]   Braroe, Niels Winther. 1975. *Indian and
White: Self-Image and Interaction in a
Canadian Plains Community.* Stanford:
Stanford University Press.   (33)

*[43]   Briggs, Jean L. 1970. "Kapluna Daugh-
ter: Living with the Eskimos." *Transaction* 7:12–24.   (26)

[44]   Brockman, C. Thomas. 1971. "Correlation of Social Class and Education on
the Flathead Indian Reservation, Montana." *Rocky Mountain Social Science
Journal* 8:11–17.   (37)

[45]   Brown, Julia S. 1952. "A Comparative
Study of Deviations from Sexual
Mores." *American Sociological Review*
17:135–46.   (9)

[46]   Brown, Kaye. 1976. "Quantitative Testing and Revitalization Behavior: On
Carroll's Explanation of the Ghost
Dance." *American Sociological Review*
41:741–44.   (24)

[47]   Browne, William P., and Michael Davis.
1976. "Community Control and the
Reservation: Self-Interest as a Factor
Limiting Reform." *Ethnicity* 3:368–77.   (43)

[48]   Burma, John H. 1963. "Interethnic
        Marriage in Los Angeles, 1948–1959."
        Social Forces 42:156–65.   (16)

[49]   Butler, Raymond V. 1978. "The
        Bureau of Indian Affairs: Activities
        since 1945." *Annals of the American
        Academy of Political and Social Science*
        436:50–60.   (30)

[50]   Carlson, Glen E. 1934. "The American
        Indian—Past and Present." *Social Sci-
        ence* 9:185–91.   (10)

[51]   Carroll, Michael P. 1975. "Revitaliza-
        tion Movements and Social Structure:
        Some Quantitative Tests." *American
        Sociological Review* 40:389–401.   (23)

[52]   ———. 1976. "Reply to Brown." *Ameri-
        can Sociological Review* 41:744–46.   (24)

[53]   ———. 1979. "Rejoinder to Lands-
        man." *American Sociological Review*
        44:166–68.   (24)

[54]   Carrothers, A. W. R. 1967. "Canada:
        Reluctant Imperalist." *Journal of Cana-
        dian Studies* 2:11–23.   (30)

[55]   Chadwick, Bruce A., and Joseph H.
        Strauss. 1975. "The Assimilation of
        American Indians into Urban Society:

The Seattle Case." *Human Organization* 34:359–70. (62)

[56] Chadwick, Bruce A., Joseph Strauss, Howard M. Bahr, and Lowell K. Halverson. 1976. "Confrontation with the Law: The Case of the American Indians in Seattle." *Phylon* 37:163–71. (63)

[57] Chadwick, Bruce A., and Lynn C. White. 1973. "Correlates of Length of Urban Residence among the Spokane Indians." *Human Organization* 32:9–16. (62)

[58] Clifton, James A. 1965. "Culture Change, Structural Stability, and Factionalism in the Prairie Potawatomi Reservation Community." *Midcontinent American Studies Journal* 6:101–23. (19)

[59] Clifton, Rodney A. 1972. "The Social Adjustment of Native Students in a Northern Canadian Hostel." *Canadian Review of Sociology and Anthropology* 9:163–66. (55)

[60] ———. 1975. "Self-Concept and Attitudes: A Comparison of Canadian Indian and Non-Indian Students." *Canadian Review of Sociology and Anthropology* 12:577–84. (59)

[61]   Clinton, Lawrence, Bruce A. Chadwick,
        and Howard M. Bahr. 1975. "Urban
        Relocation Reconsidered: Antecedents
        of Employment among Indian Males."
        Rural Sociology 40:117–33.   (60)

[62]   Cockerham, William C., and Audie L.
        Blevins, Jr. 1976. "Open School vs.
        Traditional School: Self-Identification
        among Native American and White
        Adolescents." *Sociology of Education*
        49:164–69.   (56)

[63]   ———. 1976. "Reply to Thornton and
        Marsh-Thornton." *Sociology of Education*
        49:248.   (56)

*[64]   Cohen, Fay G. 1973. "The Indian Pa-
        trol in Minneapolis: Social Control and
        Social Change in an Urban Context."
        Law and Society Review 7:779–86.   (63)

[65]   Cohen, Ronald. 1966. "Modernism and
        the Hinterland: The Canadian Exam-
        ple." *International Journal of Comparative
        Sociology* 7:52–75.   (19)

[66]   Collier, John. 1942. "The Indian in a
        Wartime Nation." *Annals of the American
        Academy of Political and Social Science*
        223:29–35.   (44)

[67]   ———. 1945. "United States Indian Administration as a Laboratory of Ethnic Relations." *Social Research* 12:265–303.   (29)

[68]   Collier, John, and Laura Thompson. 1946. "The Indian Education and Administration Research." *Sociometry* 9:141–42.   (29)

[69]   Collins, John James. 1968. "Law Function and Judicial Process at a New Mexico Pueblo." *International Journal of Comparative Sociology* 9:129–31.   (46)

[70]   ———. 1969. "Transformation of the Self and the Duplication of Ceremonial Structure." *International Journal of Comparative Sociology* 10:302–7.   (24)

[71]   Cussler, Margaret. 1946. "Film-making as a Focus of Social Forces in an Indian Tribe." *Rural Sociology* 11:362–65.   (37)

[72]   Deloria, Vine, Jr. 1978. "Legislation and Litigation concerning American Indians." *Annals of the American Academy of Political and Social Science* 436:86–96.   (30)

[73]   Denton, Trevor. 1972. "Migration from a Canadian Indian Reserve." *Journal of Canadian Studies* 7:54–62.   (63)

[74]   ———. 1975. "Canadian Indian Migrants and Impression Management of Ethnic Stigma." *Canadian Review of Sociology and Anthropology* 12:65–71.   (63)

[75]   Deprez, Paul. 1971. "The Economic Development of the Canadian North: With or without the Indians?" *Annals of Regional Science* 5:8–16.   (41)

[76]   DeRuyter, Barbara. 1976. "Ethnic Differentials in Age at First Marriage, Canada, 1971." *Journal of Comparative Family Studies* 7:159–66.   (15)

[77]   Dobyns, Henry F. 1965. "Therapeutic Experience of Responsible Democracy." *Midcontinent American Studies Journal* 6:171–86.   (43)

[78]   ———. 1976. *Native American Historical Demography: A Critical Bibliography.* Bloomington: Indiana University Press.   (13)

[79]   Dozier, Edward P., George E. Simpson, and J. Milton Yinger. 1957. "The Integration of Americans of Indian Descent." *Annuals of the American Academy of Political and Social Science* 3:158–65.   (32)

*[80]   Dryfoos, Robert J., Jr. 1970. "Two Tactics for Ethnic Survival: Eskimo and Indian." *Transaction* 7:51–54.   (21)

[81]   Dumont, Robert V., Jr., and Murray L.
         Wax. 1969. "Cherokee School Society
         and the Intercultural Classroom."
         Human Organization 28:217–26.   (54)

[82]   Dunning, R. W. 1971. "The Indian
         Situation: A Canadian Government Di-
         lemma." *International Journal of Com-
         parative Sociology* 12:128–33.   (31, 43)

[83]   Fairfield, Robert C. 1967. "New Towns
         in the Far North." *Journal of Canadian
         Studies* 2:18–26.   (31)

[84]   Feagin, Joe R., and Randal Anderson.
         1973. "Intertribal Attitudes among Na-
         tive American Youth." *Social Science
         Quarterly* 54:117–31.   (43)

*[85]   Fisher, A. D. 1969. "White Rites vs.
         Indian Rights." *Transaction* 7:29–33.   (55)

[86]   ———. 1976. "The Dialectic of Indian
         Life in Canada." *Canadian Review of
         Sociology and Anthropology* 13:458–64.   (34)

[87]   Forslund, Morris A., and Virginia A.
         Cranston. 1975. "A Self-Report Com-
         parison of Indian and Anglo Delin-
         quency in Wyoming." *Criminology*
         12:193–98.   (48)

[88]   Forslund, Morris A., and Ralph E.
         Meyers. 1974. "Delinquency among

Wind River Reservation Youth."
Criminology 12:97–106.   (48)

[89]   Fowler, Loretta. 1973. "The Arapahoe
Ranch: An Experiment in Cultural
Change and Economic Development."
*Economic Development and Cultural
Change* 21:446–64.   (42)

[90]   Fox, J. R. 1960. "Therapeutic Rituals
and Social Structure in Cochiti Pueblo."
Human Relations 13:291–303.   (50)

[91]   Francis, E. K. 1956. "Multiple Inter-
group Relations in the Upper Rio
Grande Region." *American Sociological
Review* 21:84–87.   (28)

[92]   Frideres, James S. 1975. "Prejudice
towards Minority Groups: Ethnicity or
Class." *Ethnicity* 2:34–42.   (27)

[93]   Fried, Morton H. 1952. "Land Tenure,
Geography, and Ecology in the Contact
of Cultures." *American Journal of Eco-
nomics and Sociology* 11:391–412.   (19)

*[94]   Fuchs, Estelle, and Robert J.
Havighurst. 1973. *To Live on This Earth:
American Indian Education.* Garden City,
N.Y.: Anchor Press.   (55)

[95] Funk, Sandra G., Abraham D.
      Horowitz, Raanan Lipshitz, and Forrest
      W. Young. 1976. "The Perceived Struc-
      ture of American Ethnic Groups: The
      Use of Multidimensional Scaling in
      Stereotype Research." *Sociometry*
      39:116–30.   (26)

*[96] Garbarino, Merwyn S. 1970. "Seminole
      Girl." *Transaction* 7:40–46.   (37)

[97] Gilbert, William Harlen, Jr. 1946.
      "Memorandum concerning the Char-
      acteristics of the Larger Mixed-Blood
      Racial Islands of the Eastern United
      States." *Social Forces* 24:438–47.   (38)

[98] Gillin, John. 1939. "Personality in Pre-
      literate Societies." *American Sociological
      Review* 4:681–702.   (57)

[99] Gillin, John, and Victor Raimy. 1940.
      "Acculturation and Personality." *Ameri-
      can Sociological Review* 5:371–80.   (31)

[100] Goldschmidt, Walter. 1953. "Values and
      the Field of Comparative Sociology."
      American Sociological Review 18:287–93. (4)

[101] Gouldner, Alvin W., and Richard A.
      Peterson. 1962. *Notes on Technology and
      the Moral Order*. Indianapolis: Bobbs-
      Merrill.   (9)

*[102]   Graburn, Nelson. 1967. "The Eskimo and 'Airport Art.'" *Transaction* 4:28–33.   (21)

[103]   Graves, Theodore D. 1966. "Alternative Models for the Study of Urban Migration." *Human Organization* 25:295–99.   (62)

[104]   Graves, Theodore D., and Minor Van Arsdale. 1966. "Values, Expectations and Relocation: The Navaho Migrant to Denver." *Human Organization* 25:300–307.   (62)

[105]   Grindstaff, Carl F., Wilda Galloway, and Joanne Nixon. 1973. "Racial and Cultural Identification among Canadian Indian Children." *Phylon* 34:368–77.   (59)

*[106]   Guillemin, Jeanne. 1975. *Urban Renegades: The Cultural Strategy of American Indians.* New York: Columbia University Press.   (63)

[107]   Gulick, John. 1958. "The Acculturation of Eastern Cherokee Community Organization." *Social Forces* 36:246–50.   (18)

[108]   Gundlach, James H., and Alden E. Roberts. 1978. "Native American Indian Migration and Relocation: Success

or Failure." *Pacific Sociological Review* 12:117–28. (61)

[109] Haas, Theodore H. 1957. "The Legal Aspects of Indian Affairs from 1887 to 1957." *Annals of the American Academy of Political and Social Science* 311:12–22. (30)

[110] Hackenberg, Robert A. 1966. "An Anthropological Study of the Demographic Transition: The Papago Information System." *Milbank Memorial Fund Quarterly* 44: 470–93. (13)

[111] Hadley, J. Nixon. 1957. "Demography of the American Indians." *Annals of the American Academy of Political and Social Science* 311:23–30. (11)

[112] Hall, Edwin L., and Albert A. Simkus. 1975. "Inequality in the Types of Sentences Received by Native Americans and Whites." *Criminology* 13:199–222. (48)

[113] Hallowell, A. I. 1941. "The Social Function of Anxiety in a Primitive Society." *American Sociological Review* 6:869–81. (45)

[114] Halseth, Odd S. 1926. "The Revival of Pueblo Pottery Making." *Journal of Applied Sociology* 10:533–47. (20)

[115]   Harper, Roland M. 1937. "A Statistical Study of the Croatans." *Rural Sociology* 2:444–56.   (38)

[116]   Hart, Hornell, and Donald L. Taylor. 1944. "Was There a Prehistoric Trend from Smaller to Larger Political Units?" *American Journal of Sociology* 49:289–301.   (9)

[117]   Hart, Wesley R., Jr. 1961–62. "The Urbanization of the Yankton Indians." *Human Organization* 20:226–31.   (62)

[118]   Harte, Thomas J. 1959. "Trends in Mate Selection in a Tri-racial Isolate." *Social Forces* 37:215–21.   (38)

[119]   Havighurst, Robert J. 1957. "Education among American Indians: Individual and Cultural Aspects." *Annals of the American Academy of Political and Social Science* 311: 105–15.   (53)

[120]   ——. 1978. "Indian Education since 1960." *Annals of the American Academy of Political and Social Science* 436:13–26.   (53)

[121]   Havighurst, Robert J., and Bernice L. Neugarten. 1955. *American Indian and White Children: A Sociopsychological Investigation.* Chicago: University of Chicago Press.   (57)

[122]   Hawley [Ellis], Florence. 1947. "The
        Keresan Holy Rollers: An Adaptation
        to American Individualism." *Social
        Forces* 26:272–80.   (23)

[123]   Hayner, Norman S. 1942. "Variability
        in the Criminal Behavior of American
        Indians." *American Journal of Sociology*
        47:602–13.   (23,46)

[124]   Hayner, Norman S., and Una Hayner.
        1943. "Three Generations of Pacific
        Northwest Indians." *American Sociologi-
        cal Review* 8:650–65.   (18)

[125]   Heinrich, Albert. 1972. "Divorce as an
        Integrative Social Factor among Es-
        kimos." *Journal of Comparative Family
        Studies* 3:265–72.   (50)

[126]   Helm, June. 1962. "The Ecological Ap-
        proach in Anthropology." *American
        Journal of Sociology* 67:630–96.   (4)

[127]   Herskovits, Melville, J. 1929. "Race Re-
        lations." *American Journal of Sociology*
        34:1129–39.   (27)

[128]   ———. 1930. "Race Relations." *Ameri-
        can Journal of Sociology* 35:1052–62.   (27)

[129]   ———. 1932. "Race Relations." *Ameri-
        can Journal of Sociology* 37:976–82.   (27)

[130]   Hewett, Edgar L. 1934. "The Aborigines of Southern California." *Sociology and Social Research* 18:358–64.   (10)

[131]   Hobart, Charles W. 1970. "Eskimo Education in the Canadian Arctic." *Canadian Review of Sociology and Anthropology* 7:49–69.   (54)

[132]   Hobart, Charles W., and C. S. Brant. 1966. "Eskimo Education, Danish and Canadian: A Comparison." *Canadian Review of Sociology and Anthropology* 3:47–66.   (54)

[133]   Hoebel, E. Adamson. 1941. "Law-ways of the Primitive Eskimos." *Journal of the American Institute of Criminal Law and Criminology* 31:663–83.   (45)

[134]   Holden, David E. W. 1969. "Modernization among Town and Bush Cree in Quebec." *Canadian Review of Sociology and Anthropology* 6:237–48.   (19)

[135]   Honigmann, John J. 1957. "Interpersonal Relations and Ideology in a Northern Canadian Community." *Social Forces* 35:365–70.   (26)

[136]   ———. 1965. "Social Disintegration in Five Northern Canadian Communities."

Canadian Review of Sociology and Anthropology 2:199–214.   (49)

[137]   Honigman,, John J., and Irma Honigmann. 1965. "How Baffin Island Eskimos Have Learned to Use Alcohol." *Social Forces* 44:73–83.   (49)

[138]   Humphrey, Norman D. 1942. "Police and Tribal Welfare in Plains Indian Culture." *Journal of Criminal Law and Criminology* 33:147–61.   (45)

[139]   Iverson, Peter. 1976. "Legal Assistance and Navajo Economic Revitalization." *Journal of Ethnic Studies* 4:21–34.   (40)

[140]   Janes, Robert W. 1949. "A Note on an Apparent Relationship between Temperamental Traits and Personality Traits." *Social Forces* 28:199–204.   (57)

[141]   Jayewardene, C. H. S. 1975. "Violence among the Eskimos." *Canadian Journal of Criminology and Corrections* 17:307–14.   (47)

[142]   Johnson, Guy B. 1939. "Personality in a White-Indian-Negro Community." *American Sociological Review* 4:516–23.   (38)

[143]   Johnston, Thomas F. 1976. "Alaskan Native Social Adjustment and the Role

of Eskimo and Indian Music." *Journal of Ethnic Studies* 3:21–36.   (21)

[144]   Jones, Charles F. 1953. "Notes on Indian Education." *Journal of Educational Sociology* 27:16–23.   (53)

[145]   Jones, Dorothy M. 1976. "The Mystique of Expertise in Social Service: An Alaskan Example." *Journal of Sociology and Social Welfare* 3:332–46.   (62)

[146]   ————. 1978. "Interagency Conflict, Power, and Sanctioning Systems: An Alaskan Example." *Journal of Sociology and Social Welfare* 5:435–45.   (62)

[147]   Kallen, Horace M. 1958. "On 'Americanizing' the American Indian" *Social Research* 25:469–73.   (32)

[148]   Kaplan, Bernice A. 1953. "Ethnic Identification in an Indian Mestizo Community." *Phylon* 14:179–86.   (14)

*[149]   Kehoe, Alice B. 1975. "Dakota Indian Ethnicity in Saskatchewan." *Journal of Ethnic Studies* 3:37–42.   (34)

[150]   Kelly, William H. 1957. "The Economic Basis of Indian Life." *Annals of the American Academy of Political and Social Science* 311:71–79.   (40)

[151]   Kerchoff, Alan C. 1959. "Anomie and
         Achievement Motivation: A Study of
         Personality Development within Cul-
         tural Disorganization." *Social Forces*
         37:196–202.   (58)

[152]   Kerchoff, Alan C., and Thomas C.
         McCormick. 1955. "Marginal Status
         and Marginal Personality." *Social Forces*
         34:48–55.   (58)

[153]   Kluckhohn, Clyde. 1946. "Personality
         Formation among the Navaho Indians."
         Sociometry 9:128–32.   (57)

[154]   Kunitz, Stephen J. 1974. "Factors
         Influencing Recent Navajo and Hopi
         Population Change." *Human Organiza-
         tion* 33:7–16.   (13)

[155]   Kuo, Chun-yan. 1976. "The Effect of
         Education on the Earnings of Indian,
         Eskimo, Métis, and White Workers in
         the Mackenzie District of Northern
         Canada." *Economic Development and Cul-
         tural Change* 24:387–98.   (35)

[156]   Kupferer, Harriet J. 1962. "Health
         Practices and Educational Aspirations
         as Indicators of Acculturation and So-
         cial Class among the Eastern
         Cherokee." *Social Forces* 41:154–62.   (35)

[157]   ———. 1965. "The Isolated Eastern Cherokee." *Midcontinent American
Studies Journal* 6:124–34.   (20)

[158]   Labovitz, Sanford. 1974. "Some Evi-
dence of Canadian Ethnic, Racial, and
Sexual Antagonism." *Canadian Review of
Sociology and Anthropology* 11:247–54.   (26)

[159]   LaFarge, Oliver. 1957. "Termination of
Federal Supervision: Disintegration
and the American Indian." *Annals of the
American Academy of Political and Social
Sciences* 311:41–46.   (30)

[160]   Landsman, Gail. 1979. "The Ghost
Dance and the Policy of Land Allotment." *American Sociological Review*
44:162–66.   (24)

[161]   Lavender, Abraham D., and John M.
Forsyth. 1976. "The Sociological Study
of Minority Groups as Reflected by
Leading Sociology Journals: Who Gets
Studied and Who Gets Neglected?"
Ethnicity 3:388–98.   (7)

[162]   LaViolette, Forrest E. 1961. *The Struggle for Survival: Indian Cultures and the
Protestant Ethic in British Columbia.* Toronto: University of Toronto Press.   (22)

[163]   Leighton, Dorothea C., and Clyde
Kluckhohn. 1946. *The Navaho.* Cam-

bridge, Mass,: Harvard University
Press.   (58)

[164]   Leupp, Hon. Francis E. 1909. "Indian
Lands: Their Administration with Reference to Present and Future Use." *Annals of the American Academy of Political
and Social Science* 33:620–30.   (29)

[165]   Linton, Ralph. 1940 "A Neglected Aspect of Social Organization." *American
Journal of Sociology* 45:870–86.   (36)

[166]   Lowie, Robert H. 1914. "Social Organization." *American Journal of Sociology*
20:68–97.   (49)

[167]   ———. 1915. "Psychology and Sociology." *American Journal of Sociology*
21:217–29.   (3)

[168]   ———. 1936. "Cultural Anthropology:
A Science." *American Journal of Sociology*
42:301–20.   (3)

[169]   ———. 1942. "The Transition of Civilizations in Primitive Societies." *American
Journal of Sociology* 47:527–43.   (19)

[170]   Ludeman, W. W. 1960. "The Indian
Student in College." *Journal of Educational Sociology* 33:333–35.   (54)

[171]   Lurie, Nancy Oestreich. 1957. "The Indian Claims Commission Act." *Annals of the American Academy of Political and Social Science* 311:56–70.   (30)

[172]   ———. 1978. "The Indian Claims Commission." *Annals of the American Academy of Political and Social Science* 436:97–110.   (30)

[173]   Macgregor, Gordon. 1945. *Warriors without Weapons: A Study of the Pine Ridge Sioux.* Chicago: University of Chicago Press.   (58)

[174]   McIlwraith, Thomas F. 1947. "The Indians of Canada." *Annals of the American Academy of ~Political and Social Science* 253:164–68.   (28)

[175]   McKenzie, Fayette Avery. 1914. "The Assimilation of the American Indian." *American Journal of Sociology* 19:761–72.   (6)

[176]   Maclay, Howard, and Edward E. Ware. 1961. "Cross-Cultural Use of the Semantic Differential." *Behavioral Science* 6:185–90.   (58)

[177]   MacLeod, William Christie. 1925. "Some Aspects of Primitive Chattel Slavery." *Social Forces* 4:137–41.   (36)

[178] ———. 1926. "Marriage, Divorce and Illegitimacy in a Primitive Pecuniary Culture." *Social Forces* 5:109–17. (49)

[179] ———. 1928. *The American Indian Frontier.* London: Kegan Paul. (33)

[180] ———. 1928. "Big Business and the North American Indian." *American Journal of Sociology* 34:480–91. (39)

[181] ———. 1932. "Aspects of the Earlier Development of Law and Punishment." *Journal of the American Institute of Criminal Law and Criminology* 23:169–90. (45)

[182] ———. 1934. "Law, Procedure, and Punishment in Early Bureaucracies." *Journal of the American Institute of Criminal Law and Criminology* 25:225–44. (45)

[183] ———. 1937. "Police and Punishment among Native Americans of the Plains." *Journal of the American Institute of Criminal Law and Criminology* 28:181–201. (45)

[184] McNickle, D'Arcy. 1957. "Indian and European: Indian-White Relations from Discovery to 1887." *Annals of the American Academy of Political and Social Science* 311:1–11. (28)

[185] Mail, Patricia D. 1978. "Hippocrates Was a Medicine Man: The Health Care

of Native Americans in the Twentieth Century." *Annals of the American Academy of Political and Social Science* 436:40–49.   (13)

[186]   Mandelbaum, David G. 1937. "Boom Periods in the History of an Indian Tribe." *Social Forces* 16:117–19.   (39)

[187]   March, James G. 1955. "Group Autonomy and Intergroup Control." *Social Forces* 33:322–26.   (9)

[188]   Margon, Arthur. 1976. "Indians and Immigrants: A Comparison of Groups New to the City." *Journal of Ethnic Studies* 4:17–28.   (61)

[189]   Marjoribanks, Kevin. 1972. "Ethnic and Environmental Influences on Mental Abilities." *American Journal of Sociology* 78:323–37.   (59)

[190]   Martin, Harry W. 1964. "Correlates of Adjustment among American Indians in an Urban Environment." *Human Organization* 23:290–95.   (62)

[191]   Mekeel, Scudder. 1943. "Education, Child-Training, and Culture." *American Journal of Sociology* 48:676–91.   (53)

[192]   Melling, J. 1966. "Recent Developments in Official Policy towards Canadian

Indians and Eskimos." *Race* 7:379–99. (30)

[193] Metcalf, Ann. 1976. "From Schoolgirl to Mother: The Effects of Education on Navajo Women." *Social Problems* 23:535–44. (52)

[194] Michelson, Truman. 1929. "The Changing Character of Fox Adoption-Feasts." *American Journal of Sociology* 34:890–92. (39)

[195] Minnis, Mhyra S. 1962. "Selected Social Problems of Fort Hall Reservation." *Sociology and Social Research* 46:436–45. (48)

[196] ———. 1963. "The Relationship of the Social Structure of an Indian Community to Adult and Juvenile Delinquency." *Social Forces* 41:395–403. (48)

[197] Mooney, James. 1928. "The Aboriginal Population of America North of Mexico." *Smithsonian Miscellaneous Collections* 80:1–40. (12)

[198] Mumford, Eben. 1907. "The Origins of Leadership, III." *American Journal of Sociology* 12:500–31. (36)

[199]   Muntz, E. E. 1925. "Civilization and Its
         Effect on Indian Character." *Social
         Forces* 4:131–36.   (19)

[200]   Murphy, Joseph A., M.D. 1911.
         "Health Problems of the Indians." *An-
         nals of the American Academy of Political
         and Social Science* 37:347–53.   (13)

*[201]   Neff, Ronald L., and Jay A. Weinstein.
         1975. "Iowa's Indians Come of Age."
         Society 12:22–26.   (44)

*[202]   Officer, James E. 1970. "A New Image
         for the Great White Father." *Midconti-
         nent American Studies Journal* 11:5–
         19.   (30)

[203]   ———. 1978. "The Bureau of Indian
         Affairs since 1945: An Assessment."
         *Annals of the American Academy of Politi-
         cal and Social Science* 436:61–72.   (30)

[204]   Olson, Dean F. 1969. "Territory, Vil-
         lage Identity, and the Modern Eskimo
         Reindeer Manager." *Canadian Review of
         Sociology and Anthropology* 6:248–57.   (37)

[205]   Opler, Marvin K. 1943. "Women's So-
         cial Status and the Forms of Marriage."
         American Journal of Sociology 49:125–
         46.   (51)

[206]   ———. 1955. "The Influence of Ethnic and Class Subcultures on Child Care." *Social Problems* 3:12–20.   (51)

[207]   Opler, Morris Edward. 1945. "Themes as Dynamic Forces in Culture." *American Journal of Sociology* 51:198–206.   (17)

[208]   Osgood, Charles E. 1960. "The Cross-Cultural Generality of Visual-Verbal Synesthetic Tendencies." *Behavioral Science* 5:146–69.   (58)

[209]   Paige, Karen E., and Jeffrey M. Paige. 1973. "The Politics of British Practices: A Strategic Analysis." *American Sociological Review* 38:663–77.   (9)

[210]   Palmer, Edward Nelson. 1948. "Culture Contacts and Population Growth." *American Journal of Sociology* 53:258–62.   (11)

[211]   Palys, Theodore S. 1976. "An Assessment of Legal and Culture Stigma regarding Unskilled Workers." *Canadian Journal of Criminology and Corrections* 18:247–57.   (47)

[212]   Panunzio, Constantine. 1942. "Intermarriage in Los Angeles, 1924–33." *American Journal of Sociology* 47:690–701.   (16)

[213]   Panzarella, Robert, and Ansley LaMar. 1979. "Attitudes of Blacks and Whites toward Native American Revolutionary Tactics for Social Change." *Human Relations* 32:69–75.   (44)

[214]   Parenton, Vernon J., and Roland J. Pellegrin. 1950. "The 'Sabines': A Study of Racial Hybrids in a Louisiana Coastal Parish." *Social Forces* 29:148–54.   (38)

[215]   Parker, Arthur C. 1916. "The Social Elements of the Indian Problem." *American Journal of Sociology* 22:252–67.   (29)

[216]   Passel, Jeffrey. 1976. "Provisional Evaluation of the 1970 Census Count of American Indians." *Demography* 13:397–409.   (16)

[217]   Peterson, Helen L. 1957. "American Indian Political Participation." *Annals of the American Academy of Political and Social Science* 311:116–26.   (44)

[218]   Peterson, William. 1975. "A Demographer's View of Prehistoric Demography." *Current Anthropology* 16:227–45.   (12)

[219]   Pettit, Donald E. 1965. "A Study of Aspiration among Three Cultural

Groups of Prisoners." *Canadian Journal of Corrections* 7:112–16.   (46)

[220]   Photiadis, John D. 1963. "Critical Examination of Change Programs in the Light of a System in Equilibrium." *Rural Sociology* 28:352–63.   (18)

[221]   Piche, Victor, and M. V. George. 1973. "Estimates of Vital Rates for the Canadian Indians, 1960–1970." *Demography* 10:367–82.   (15)

[222]   Porter, Frank W., III. 1979. *Indians in Maryland and Delaware: A Critical Bibliography*. Bloomington: Indiana University Press.   (39)

[223]   Price, John A. 1968. "The Migration and Adaptation of American Indians to Los Angeles." *Human Organization* 27:168–75.   (63)

[224]   Reddy, Indira I., and P. Krishnan. 1976. "Ethnic Differentials in Age at First Marriage, Canada 1961." *Journal of Comparative Family Studies* 7:55–63.   (15)

[225]   Renaud, E. B. 1926. "Evolution of Population and Dwelling in the Indian Southwest." *Social Forces* 7:263–70.   (17)

[226]   ———. 1931. "Influence of Food on Indian Culture." *Social Forces* 10:97–101.   (39)

[227]   Rhyne, Jennings J. 1930. "Community Organization in an Indian Settlement." *Social Forces* 9:95–99.   (17)

[228]   Riddell, William Renwick. 1922. "The Sad Tale of an Indian Wife." *Journal of the American Academy of Criminal Law and Criminology* 13:82–89.   (46)

[229]   ———. 1929. "The Administration of Criminal Law in the Far North of Canada." *Journal of the American Institute of Criminal Law and Criminology* 20:294–302.   (46)

[230]   Rietz, Robert W. 1953. "Leadership, Initiative and Economic Progress on an American Indian Reservation." *Economic Development and Cultural Change* 2:60–70.   (43)

[231]   Ritt, Leonard G. 1979. "Some Social and Political Views of American Indians." *Ethnicity* 6:45–72.   (44)

[232]   Robertson, R. G. 1967. "The Coming Crisis in the North." *Journal of Canadian Studies* 2:3–11.   (41)

[233]   Romaniuk, A. 1974. "Modernization

and Fertility: The Case of the James Bay Indians." *Canadian Review of Sociology and Anthropology* 11:344–59.   (15)

[234]   Romaniuk, A., and Victor Piche. 1972. "Natality Estimates for the Canadian Indians by Stable Population Models, 1900–1969." *Canadian Review of Sociology and Anthropology* 9:1–20.   (14)

[235]   Rosenblatt, Paul C. 1971. "Communication in the Practice of Love Magic." *Social Forces* 49:482–87.   (9)

[236]   Roy, Prodipto. 1962. "The Measurement of Assimilation: The Spokane Indians." *American Journal of Sociology* 67:541–51.   (31)

[237]   Ruffing, Lorraine Turner. 1976. "Navajo Economic Development Subject to Cultural Restraints." *Economic Development and Cultural Change* 24:611–21.   (40)

[238]   Sasaki, Tom T. 1956. "Sociocultural Problems in Introducing New Technology on a Navaho Irrigation Project." *Rural Sociology* 21:307–10.   (40)

[239]   ———. 1958. "Situational Changes and the Fruitland Navaho." *Journal of Social Issues* 14:17–24.   (40)

[240]   Savage, William W., Jr. 1974. "Monologues in Red and White: Contemporary Racial Attitudes in Two Southern Plains Communities." *Journal of Ethnic Studies* 2:24–31.   (26)

[241]   Schmid, Calvin F., and Charles E. Nobbe. 1965. "Socioeconomic Differentials among Non-white Races." *American Sociological Review* 30:909–22.   (35)

[242]   Schuessler, Karl F., and Harold Driver. 1956. "A Factor Analysis of Sixteen Primitive Societies." *American Sociological Review* 21:493–99.   (17)

[243]   Schusky, Ernest L. 1970. "An Indian Dilemma." *International Journal of Comparative Sociology* 11:58–66.   (34)

[244]   Sears, Louis Martin. 1916. "The Puritan and His Indian Ward." *American Journal of Sociology* 22:80–93.   (28)

[245]   Shimkin, D. B. 1955. "The Economy of a Trapping Center: The Case of Fort Yukon, Alaska." *Economic Development and Cultural Change* 3:219–40.   (40)

[246]   Siegel, Bernard J. 1955. "High Anxiety Levels and Cultural Integration: Notes on a Psycho-cultural Hypothesis." *Social Forces* 34:42–48.   (21)

[247] ———. 1965. "Social Disorganization in Picuris Pueblo." *International Journal of Comparative Sociology* 6:199–206. (18)

[248] ———. 1970. "Defensive Structuring and Environmental Stress." *American Journal of Sociology* 76:11–32. (21)

[249] Simons, Sarah E. 1902. "Social Assimilation. Part II. Illustrations—Concluded." *American Journal of Sociology* 7:539–56. (31)

[250] Simpson, George E., and J. Milton Yinger, eds. 1957. "American Indians and American Life." *Annals of the American Academy of Political and Social Science* 311:1–165. (30)

[251] Smaby, Beverly P. 1975. "The Mormons and the Indians: Conflicting Ecological Systems in the Great Basin." *American Studies* 16:35–48. (28)

[252] Smith, Mapheus. 1935. "A Comparative Study of Indian Student Leaders and Followers." *Social Forces* 13:418–26. (37)

[253] Smith, Russell Gordon. 1929. "The Concept of the Cultural Area." *Social Forces* 7:421–32. (17)

[254]   Sorkin, Alan L. 1969. "Some Aspects of American Indian Migration." *Social Forces* 48:243–50.   (60)

[255]   ———. 1971. *American Indians and Federal Aid.* Washington, D.C.: Brookings Institution.   (42)

[256]   ———. 1973. "Business and Industrial Development on American Indian Reservations." *Annals of Regional Science* 7:115–29.   (42)

[257]   ———. 1978. "The Economic Basis of Indian Life. *Annals of the American Academy of Political and Social Science* 436:1–12.   (42)

[258]   ———. 1978. *The Urban American Indian.* Lexington, Mass.: Lexington Books.   (4, 64)

[259]   Spalding, Henry S. 1929. "The Ethnologic Value of the Jesuit Relations." *American Journal of Sociology* 34:882–89.   (4)

[260]   Spindler, George D., and Louise S. Spindler. 1957. "American Indian Personality Types and Their Sociocultural Roots." *Annals of the American Academy of Political and Social Science* 311:147–57.   (57)

[261] ———. 1978. "Identity, Militancy and Cultural Congruence: The Menominee and Kainai." *Annals of the American Academy of Political and Social Science* 436:73–85. (22)

[262] Stanley, Sam, and Robert K. Thomas. 1978. "Current Social and Demographic Trends among North American Indians." *Annals of the American Academy of Political and Social Science* 436:111–20. (11)

[263] Stephan, G. Edward, and Stephen M. Wright. 1973. "Indian Tribal Territories in the Pacific Northwest: A Cross-Cultural Test of the Size-Density Hypothesis." *Annals of Regional Science* 7:113–23. (12)

[264] Stern, Bernhard J. 1928. "Lewis Henry Morgan: American Ethnologist." *Social Forces* 6:344–57. (3)

[265] ———. 1929. "An Indian Shaker Initiation and Healing Service." *Social Forces* 7:432–34. (24, 51)

[266] Strodtbeck, Fred L. 1951. "Husband-Wife Interaction over Revealed Differences." *American Sociological Review* 16:468–73. (51)

[267]   Tax, Sol. 1978. "The Impact of Urbani-
        zation on American Indians." *Annals of
        the American Academy of Political and So-
        cial Science* 436:121–36.   (61)

[268]   Tefft, Stanton K. 1967. "Anomy, Val-
        ues, and Culture Change among
        Teen-age Indians: An Exploratory
        Study." *Sociology of Education* 40:145–
        57.   (59)

[269]   ———. 1971. "Task Experience and In-
        tertribal Value Differences on the Wind
        River Reservation." *Social Forces*
        49:604–13.   (59)

[270]   Thomas, Robert K. 1961. "The Red-
        bird Smith Movement." *United States
        Bureau of American Ethnology Bulletin*
        180:161–66.   (24)

[271]   ———. 1965. "Pan-Indianism." *Mid-
        continent American Studies Journal* 6:75–
        83.   (42)

[272]   ———. 1967. "The Role of the Church
        in Indian Adjustment." *Kansas Journal
        of Sociology* 3:20–28.   (23)

[273]   Thomas, William I. 1898. "The Rela-
        tion of Sex to Primitive Social Control."
        American Journal of Sociology 3:754–
        76.   (3)

[274] ———. 1899. "Sex in Primitive Industry." *American Journal of Sociology* 4:474–88. (3)

[275] Thompson, Hildegard. 1957. "Education among American Indians: Institutional Aspects." *Annals of the American Academy of Political and Social Science* 311:95–104. (53)

[276] Thompson, Laura, and Alice Joseph. 1944. *The Hopi Way*. Chicago: University of Chicago Press. (58)

[277] ———. 1947. "White Pressures on Indian Personality and Culture." *American Journal of Sociology* 53:17–22. (18)

[278] Thornton, Russell. 1977. "American Indian Studies as an Academic Discipline." *Journal of Ethnic Studies* 5.1–15. (5)

[279] ———. 1978. "Implications of Catlin's American Indian Population Estimates for Revision of Mooney's Estimate." *American Journal of Physical Anthropology* 49:11–14. (12)

[280] ———. 1979. "American Indian Historical Demography: A Review Essay with Suggestions for Future Research." *American Indian Culture and Research Journal* 3:69–74. (13)

[281]   Thornton, Russell, and Mary K. Grasmick. 1979. *Bibliography of Social Science
Research and Writings on American Indians.* Minneapolis: University of Minnesota, Center for Urban and Regional
Affairs.   (2)

[282]   ———. 1979. "Sociological Study of
American Indians: A Research Note on
Journal Literature." *Ethnicity* 6:299–
305.   (2)

[283]   Thornton, Russell, and Joan Marsh-
Thornton. 1976. "On 'Open school vs.
Traditional school: Self-Identification
among Native American and White
Adolescents'." *Sociology of Education*
49:247–48.   (56)

[284]   Tobin, Patricia L., William B. Clifford,
R. David Mustian, and A. Clarke Davis.
1975. "Value of Children and Fertility
Behavior in a Tri-racial, Rural County."
Journal of Comparative Family Studies
6:46–55.   (15)

[285]   Trosper, Ronald L. 1976. "Native
American Boundary Maintenance: The
Flathead Indian Reservation, Montana,
1860–1970." *Ethnicity* 3:256–74.   (43)

[286]   Tyroler, Herman A., and Ralph Patrick. 1972. "Epidemiologic Studies of

Papago Indian Mortality." *Human Organization* 31:163–70. (14)

[287] Udy, Stanley H., Jr. 1958. "'Bureaucratic' Elements in Organizations: Some Research Findings." *American Sociological Review* 23:415–18. (9)

[288] ———. 1959. *Organization of Work.* New Haven, Conn.: Human Relations Area Files Press. (9)

[289] Uhlmann, Julie M. 1972. "The Impact of Modernization upon Papago Indian Fertility." *Human Organization* 31:149–62. (14)

*[290] Underhill, Ruth M. 1942. "Child Training in an Indian Tribe." *Marriage and Family Living* 4:80–81.

[291] ———. 1957. "Religion among American Indians." *Annals of the American Academy of Political and Social Science* 311:127–36. (50)

[292] Upton, L. F. S. 1973. "The Origins of Canadian Indian Policy." *Journal of Canadian Studies* 8:51–61. (31)

[293] Voget, Fred. 1956. "The American Indian in Transition: Reformation and Status Innovations." *American Journal of Sociology* 62:369–78. (24)

[294]   ———. 1961. "Comment on Robert K. Thomas' 'The Redbird Smith Movement.'" *United States Bureau of American Ethnology Bulletin* 180:169–71.   (25)

[295]   Vogt, Evon Z. 1957. "The Acculturation of American Indians." *Annals of the American Academy of Political and Social Science* 311:137–46.   (32)

[296]   Von Hentig, Hans. 1945. "The Delinquency of the American Indian." *Journal of Criminal Law and Criminology* 36:75–84.   (46)

[297]   Waddell, Jack O., and O. Michael Watson, eds. 1971. *The American Indian in Urban Society.* Boston: Little, Brown.   (63)

[298]   Wahrhaftig, Albert L. 1968. "The Tribal Cherokee Population of Eastern Oklahoma." *Current Anthropology* 9:510–18.   (14)

*[299]   Wahrhaftig, Albert L., and Robert K. Thomas. 1969. "Renaissance and Repression: The Oklahoma Cherokee." *Transaction* 6:42–48.   (32)

[300]   Walker, Deward E., Jr. 1965. "Some Limitations of the Renascence Concept in Acculturation: The Nez Perce Case." *Midcontinent American Studies Journal* 6:135–48.   (20)

*[301]   ———, ed. 1972. *The Emergent Native Americans: A Reader in Culture Contact.* Boston: Little, Brown.   (33)

[302]   Wallace, Anthony F. C. 1952. "Handsome Lake and the Great Revival in the West." *American Quarterly* 4:149–64.   (24)

[303]   ———. 1952. "Individual Differences and Cultural Uniformities." *American Sociological Review* 17:747–50.   (57)

[304]   Walter, John P. 1974. "Two Poverties Equal Many Hungry Indians: An Economic and Social Study of Nutrition." *American Journal of Economics and Sociology* 33:33–44.   (35)

[305]   Watkins, Arthur V. 1957. "Termination of Federal Supervision: The Removal of Restrictions over Indian Property and Person." *Annals of the American Academy of Political and Social Science* 311:47–55.   (30)

[306]   Watson, Walter T. 1929. "A New Census and an Old Theory: Division of Labor in the Preliterate World." *American Journal of Sociology* 34:632–52.   (9)

[307]   Watters, Mary. 1927. "The Penitentes: A Folk-Observance." *Social Forces* 6:253–56.   (22)

[308]   Wax, Murray L. 1968. "The White Man's Burdensome 'Business': A Review Essay on the Change and Constancy of Literature on the American Indian." *Social Problems* 16:106– 13.   (4)

*[309]   ———. 1971. *Indian Americans: Unity and Diversity.* Englewood Cliffs, N.J.: Prentice-Hall.   (33)

[310]   Wax, Murray L., and Robert W. Buchanan, eds. 1975. *Solving "The Indian Problem": The White Man's Burdensome Business.* New York: New Viewpoints.   (31)

[311]   Wax, Murray L., and Rosalie H. Wax. 1978. "Religion among American Indians." *Annals of the American Academy of Political and Social Science* 436:27– 39.   (22)

[312]   Wax, Murray L., Rosalie H. Wax, and Robert V. Dumont, Jr. 1964. "Formal Education in an American Indian Community." *Social Problems* 11 (Supplement):1– 126.   (55)

*[313]   Wax, Rosalie H. 1967. "The Warrior Dropouts." *Transaction* 4:40– 46.   (55)

[314]   Wax, Rosalie H., and Robert K. Thomas. 1961. "American Indians and White People." *Phylon* 22:305– 17.   (26)

[315] Wax, Rosalie H., and Murray L. Wax. 1965. "Indian Education for What?" *Midcontinent American Studies Journal* 6:164–70. (55)

[316] Westermeyer, Joseph J. 1973. "Indian Powerlessness in Minnesota." *Society* 10:45–47, 50–52. (62)

[317] Weston, Warren. 1965. "Freedom of Religion and the American Indian." *Rocky Mountain Social Science Journal* 2:1–6. (34)

[318] Wilkie, Jane Riblett. 1976. "The United States Population by Race and Urban-Rural Residence 1790–1870: Reference Tables." *Demography* 13:139–48. (12)

[319] Williams, Thomas Rhys 1958 "The Structure of the Socialization Process in Papago Society." *Social Forces* 36:251–56. (51)

[320] Wilson, C. Roderick. 1969. "Papago Indian Population Movement: An Index of Cultural Change." *Rocky Mountain Social Science Journal* 6:23–32. (14)

[321] Wilson, H. Clyde, and Leo J. Wolfe. 1961. "The Relationship between Unearned Income and Individual Productive Effort on the Jicarilla Apache In-

dian Reservation." *Economic Development and Cultural Change* 9:589–97.   (41)

[322]   Wissler, Clark. 1916. "Aboriginal Maize Culture as a Typical Cultural-Complex." *American Journal of Sociology* 21:656–61.   (39)

[323]   Witt, Shirley Hill. 1965. "Nationalistic Trends among American Indians." *Midcontinent American Studies Journal* 6:51–74.   (39, 42)

[324]   Wood, Arthur Lewis. 1947. "Minority-Group Criminality and Cultural Integration." *Journal of Criminal Law and Criminology* 37:498–510.   (49)

[325]   Wood, Margaret Mary. 1943. "The Russian Creoles of Alaska as a Marginal Group." *Social Forces* 22:204–8.   (38)

[326]   Woofter, T. J., Jr. 1931. "Race Relations." *American Journal of Sociology* 36:1039–44.   (27)

[327]   Yinger, J. Milton, and George Eaton Simpson. 1978. "The Integration of Americans of Indian Descent." *Annals of the American Academy of Political and Social Science* 436:137–51.   (32)

[328] ———, eds. 1978. "American Indians Today." *Annals of the American Academy of Political and Social Sciences* 436.　　(30, 32)

[329] Young, Frank W. 1970. "Reactive Subsystems." *American Sociological Review* 35:297–307.　　(24)

[330] Zentner, Henry. 1973. *The Indian Identity Crises.* Calgary: Strayer Publications. (27)

[331] Zimmerman, William, Jr. 1957. "The Role of the Bureau of Indian Affairs since 1933." *Annals of the American Academy of Political and Social Science* 311:31–40.　　(30)